# FRANKLIN COUNTY, OHIO ADOPTIONS

## 1852-1901

Compiled by
**W. Louis Phillips, C.G.**

HERITAGE BOOKS
2007

**HERITAGE BOOKS**
*AN IMPRINT OF HERITAGE BOOKS, INC.*

**Books, CDs, and more—Worldwide**

For our listing of thousands of titles see our website
at
www.HeritageBooks.com

Published 2007 by
HERITAGE BOOKS, INC.
Publishing Division
65 East Main Street
Westminster, Maryland 21157-5026

Other books by the author:

*Annotated Bibliography of Ohio Patriots: Revolutionary War and War of 1812*

*Annual Report of the Secretary of State to the Governor of Ohio 1856:*
*Returns on the Names of Deaf and Dumb, Blind, Insane, and Idiotic Persons*

*Index to Franklin County, Ohio Guardianships and Estates, 1803-1850*

*Index to Ohio Pensioners of 1883*

*Jurisdictional Histories for Ohio's Eighty-eight Counties, 1788-1985*

*Ohio City and County Directories: The Ohio Historical Society Collection*

*Warren County, Ohio Apprenticeship and Indenture Records, 1824-1832 and 1864-1867*

*Washington County, Northwest Territory Court of Common Pleas Index, 1795-1803*

International Standard Book Number: 978-1-55613-093-9

# INTRODUCTION

In Ohio, the legal procedure of adopting children was authorized on 29 March 1859 by an act of the General Assembly. The first adoption in Franklin County occurred on 27 July 1859 when James Rice, aged 3 years, son of Jeremiah and Mary Ann Rice, was adopted by John J. and Lydia Wilson.

For the period of 1859 through 1901, there were approximately three hundred and forty adoptions in Franklin County (see accompanying graph). All of these appear in the Probate Court Journals and most of them appear in the Probate Court Complete Record, but not all. It is also recommended that the case files or packets be examined for more details. All of these records are available on microfilm or as originals at the Ohio Historical Society in Columbus.

On 26 January 1987, Judge Richard B. Metcalf of the Franklin County Probate Court sent a letter to Dennis East, State Archivist, in which instructions were contained regarding the opening of all Franklin County adoption records prior to 1 January 1926. Also, all adoption records between 1 January 1926 and 1 January 1964 if intermingled with other Probate Court records; if not intermingled, such records to be closed.

If a researcher does not find his person of interest in the following abstracts, and has good reason to believe he should have, it is strongly recommended that he examine the separate indexes in the volumes of the Journals. The researcher should also consult *General Index to Civil Dockets, 1860-1897* (later volumes also available), which is more or less a master index to the Journals, Complete Records and Civil Dockets and is available at the Franklin County Probate Court. Unfortunately, the Civil Dockets prior to 1900 have been discarded, but this presents no great loss to researchers. The most informative material appears in the Journals and Complete Records. Using the *General Index to Civil Dockets* is the best means of acquiring the case numbers for adoptions.

As an example, the adoption records for James Rice as found in the Complete Record and Journal follows:

Complete Record Vol. 3, pp. 9-11
In the matter of James Rice, Petition for Adoption. At a Court of Probate held within and for the County of Franklin on the 27th day of July A.D. 1859 in the City of Columbus before H. B. Albery, Judge of said Court, the following among other proceedings were heard:

Be it remembered that on this the 27th day of July 1859, the consent of Mary Ann Rice and the Petition of John J. Wilson and Lydia Wilson his wife praying for the adoption of James Rice into the family of John J. Wilson was filed in this office in words and figures following, to wit:

July 17, 1859.

The undersigned hereby gives her consent that John J. Wilson shall adopt and raise her son, James Rice, aged three years.

Attest: William Jamison

her
Mary Ann X Rice
mark

To the Probate Court of Franklin County, Ohio, your petitioners John J. Wilson and Lydia Wilson his wife of Franklin County, Ohio, in accordance with the statute in such cases made and provided ask leave to adopt James Rice of said County aged three yeras, a minor child not theirs by birth, but the child of Mary Ann Rice, widow of Jeremiah Rice deceased, and for a change of the name of said child to James Wilson and for such order in the premises as may be required by statute, etc.

Attest:  H. B. Albery

John J. Wilson
her
Lydia  X  Wilson
mark

Thereupon on the filing of the foregoing consent and petition, the Court ordered as follows to wit:

Probate Court July 27th, A.D. 1859.

In the matter of the adoption of James Rice by John J. Wilson and Lydia Wilson his wife.

Be it remembered that on this 27th day of July A.D. 1859, John J. Wilson an inhabitant of the State of Ohio residing in Franklin County and Lydia Wilson wife of said John J. Wilson, filed in this Court their petition for leave to adopt James Rice aged three years not theirs by birth, a child of Mary Ann Rice, widow of Jeremiah Rice late of said county aforesaid, and for a change of the name of such child to James Wilson, and produced also before this Court the written consent of Mary Ann Rice, the mother of said child, and only surviving parent, to the adoption thereof a prayer in the petition. Thereupon this matter came on to be heard and the court having examined the said Lydia Wilson wife of said John J. Wilson separate and apart from her said husband and being satisfied from such examination that the said Lydia Wilson of her own free will and accord desires such adoption, and the Court being further fully satisfied that the said petitioners have the ability to bring up and educate said child properly, and being also fully advised in the premises, and being satisfied that the adoption is fit and proper -- it is therefore now here ordered and declared by the Court that from and after this day said child is to all legal intents and purposes the child of the petitioners John J. Wilson and Lydia Wilson according to the statute in such cases made and provided, and the name of said child is hereby changed from James Rice to James Wilson.

Herman B. Albery
Probate Judge

Journal Vol. 3, page 486

In the matter of the adoption of James Rice by John J. Wilson and Lydia Wilson his wife.

Be it remembered that on this 27th day of July A.D. 1859, John J. Wilson an inhabitant of the State of Ohio residing in Franklin County, and Lydia Wilson wife of said John J. Wilson, filed in this Court their petition for leave to adopt James Rice aged three years, not theirs by birth, a child of Mary Ann Rice, widow of Jeremiah Rice late of said County deceased, and for a change of the name of such child to James Wilson, and produced also before the Court the written consent of Mary Ann Rice the mother of said child, and only surviving parent, to the adoption thereof as prayed in the petition -- Thereupon this matter came on to be heard and the Court having examined the said Lydia Wilson, wife of said John J. Wilson, separate and apart from her said husband, and being satisfied from such examination that the said Lydia Wilson of her own free will and accord desires such adoption, and the Court being further fully satisfied that the said petitioners have the ability to bring up and educate said child properly, and being also fully advised in the premises, and satisfied that the adoption is fit and proper.

It is therefore now here ordered and declared by the Court that from and after this day said child is to all legal intents and purposes the child of the petitioners, John J. Wilson and Lydia Wilson according to the Statute in such cases made and provided. And the name of said child is hereby changed from James Rice to James Wilson.

Herman B. Albery
Probate Judge

## ABBREVIATIONS

CR – Complete Record
D – Day
FR Co – Franklin County
J – Journal
M – Month
W – Week
Y – Year

Number of Adoptions in Franklin
County, OH, by Years, 1859-1901.

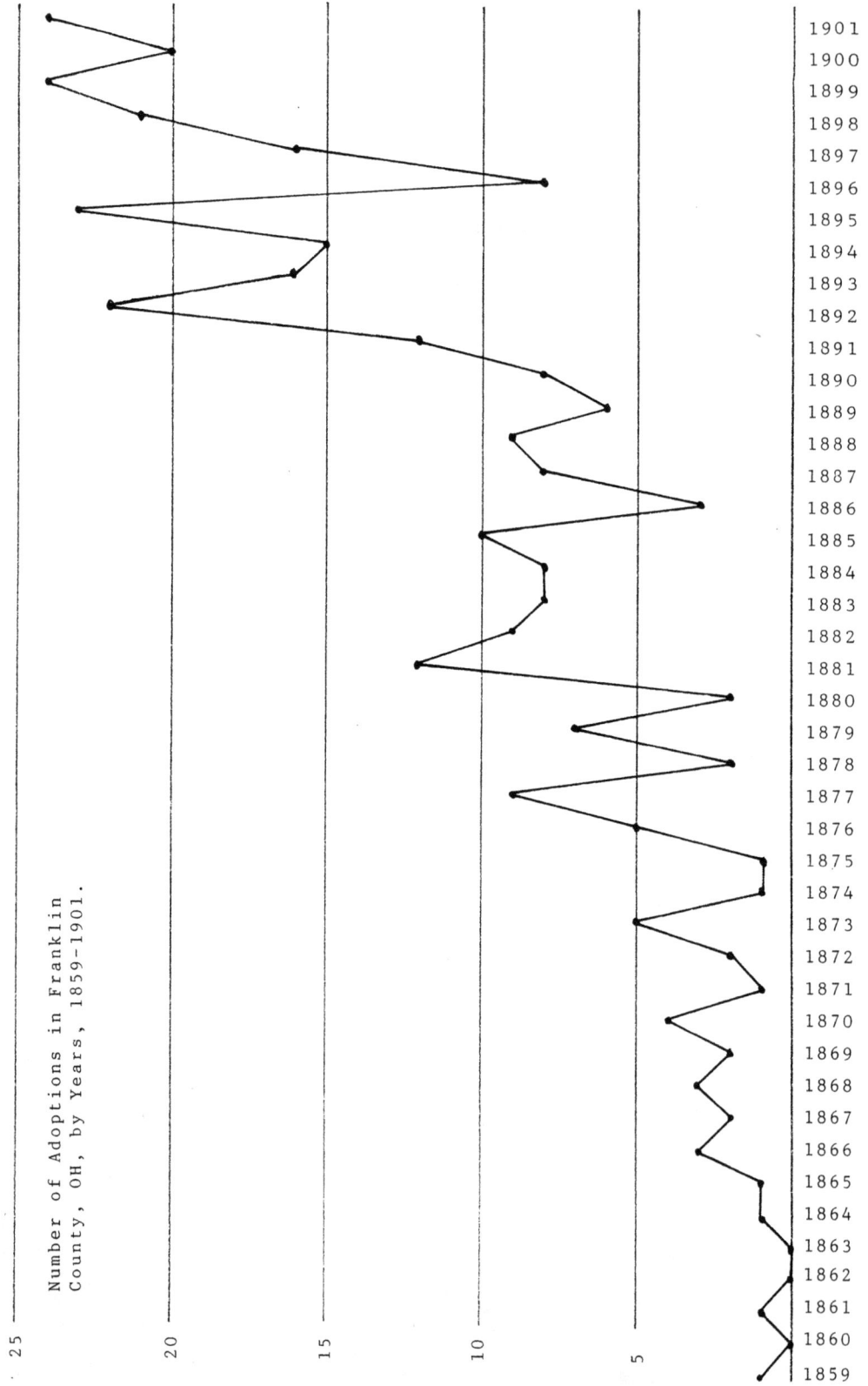

25

20

15

10

5

1901
1900
1899
1898
1897
1896
1895
1894
1893
1892
1891
1890
1889
1888
1887
1886
1885
1884
1883
1882
1881
1880
1879
1878
1877
1876
1875
1874
1873
1872
1871
1870
1869
1868
1867
1866
1865
1864
1863
1862
1861
1860
1859

adoptee:    James Rice aged 3Y of FR Co
parents:    Mary Ann Rice, widow of Jeremiah Rice late
            of FR Co
adopters:   John J & Lydia Wilson of FR Co
new name:   James Wilson
references: CR 3: 9          J 3: 486
date:       27 Jul 1859
    *
adoptee:    female child, name unknown, aged ca 5M
parents:    unknown, father dead according to a stranger
adopters:   Jacob William & Catherine Elizabeth Hummer-
            ich of Columbus
new name:   Catherine Elizabeth Hummerich
references: CR 3: 432        J 5: 170
date:       22 Nov 1861
    *
adoptee:    Lenia Glendora Garner aged 5Y on 5 Jul 1864
parents:    John S & Julia H Garner
adopters:   D H & Sallie A Royce
new name:   Lenia Glendora Royce
references:              J 7: 230
            (see J 9: 161 for reversal)
date:       24 Aug 1864
    *
adoptee:    _____ Murphy aged 1Y on or about 16 Nov
            1864
parents:    _____ Murphy (mother)
adopters:   Huldreich & Frederika Langlotz
new name:   Mary Louisa Langlotz
references:              J 7: 303
date:       5 Nov 1864
    *
adoptee:    Georgiana Young aged 2-3Y
parents:    Hannah Charlotte Young
adopters:   William S & Mary E Henry of FR Co
new name:   Georgiana Henry
references:              J 7: 371
            (see J 8: 251 for reversal)
date:       7 Jan 1865
    *
adoptee:    Margaret or Margaretha Weidenkopf aged 19Y
            came to America with Andrew Weidenkopf &
            has been living with him for several years
parents:    Elizabeth Weidenkopf (sister of Andrew)
            Elizabeth of Frankenthal, Rheinphalz, Bavaria
adopters:   Andrew & Gertrude Weidenkopf of Columbus
new name:   no name change
references:              J 8: 243
date:       4 Jan 1866
    *
adoptee:    Georgiana Henry, formerly Georgiana Young
parents:    Hannah Charlotte Young
adopters:   William S & Mary E Henry of FR Co

                         William S Henry died 14 Dec 1865, wife
                         unable to keep Georgiana, adoption reversed
new name:                name changed back to Georgiana Young
references:                             J 8: 251
                         (see J 7: 371)
date:                    13 Jan 1866
     *

adoptee:                 Emeline Eason aged 10Y on 17 Jan 1866
parents:                 unknown
adopters:                Margaretta C Fry of FR Co
new name:                Ida C Fry
references:                             J 8: 374
date:                    4 Apr 1866
     *

adoptee:                 Ida Elizabeth Ryan aged 2Y 9M 13D
parents:                 Ellen Ryan
adopters:                John William & Elizabeth M Schneider
new name:                Ida Elizabeth Schneider
references:                             J 9: 57
date:                    24 Dec 1866
     *

adoptee:                 Mary E Fristoe, a minor child (no age)
parents:                 none given
adopters:                Joshua & Nancy Mason
new name:                Mary E Mason
references:                             J 9: 89
date:                    26 Jan 1867
     *

adoptee:                 Lenia Glendora Royce, formerly Lenia Glen-
                         dora Garner
parents:                 John S & Julia H Garner
adopters:                D H & Sallie A Royce, adoption being reversed
new name:                name changed back to Lenia Glendora Garner
references:                             J 9: 161
                         (see J 7: 230)
date:                    19 Mar 1867
     *

adoptee:                 Fannie B & Elizabeth D Wharton (no ages)
parents:                 Jane Houston, formerly Jane Wharton
                         Robert J Wharton, father, dead
adopters:                Alexander & Jane Houston
new name:                Fannie Brooks Houston & Elizabeth Dunn
                         Houston
references:                             J 9: 438
date:                    22 Oct 1867
     *

adoptee:                 Albert Gordon (no age)
parents:                 none given
adopters:                John Bethel
new name:                Albert Bethel
references:                             J 10: 23
date:                    14 Mar 1868
     *

adoptee:     Joseph Jackson aged 10Y on 15(?) May 1868
parents:     Joseph Jackson, deceased, Susan Jackson,
             widow
adopters:    P & Mary B Campbell
new name     Joseph Campbell
references:                      J 10: 246
date:        4 Dec 1868 (5 Oct 1865)
    *

adoptee:     William Taylor aged 4M as of 28 Apr 1866
parents:     Charles & Electa Taylor
adopters:    James B & Eliza Jane Rusk
new name:    William Rusk
references:                      J 10: 246
date:        4 Dec 1868 (28 Apr & 28 June 1866)
    *

adoptee:     Charles Krell aged 18Y
parents:     father deceased (not named), mother
             Sabina Bickel
adopters:    John G & Sabina Bickel
new name:    Charles Bickel
references:                      J 10: 428
date:        2 Aug 1869
    *

adoptee:     Frances Alley aged 13Y
parents:     Eleanor Gill
adopters:    Harriet Gray
new name:    Frances Gray
references:                      J 10: 499
date:        8 Nov 1869
    *

adoptee:     Margaret Scanlan aged 5Y
parents:     Bartholomew Scanlan, mother dead
adopters:    George & Catherine Burck of FR Co
new name:    Margaret Josephine Burck
references:                      J 11: 13
date:        9 Mar 1870
    *

adoptee:     Ida Hall aged ca 4½M
parents:     Henry M & Mary Hall
adopters:    Ephraim & Ella R Dallas
new name:    Ida Blanch(e) Dallas
references:                      J 11: 82
date:        5 Jul 1870
    *

adoptee:     Rosana E Johnson aged 8Y on 17 Nov 1871
parents:     Mary Ann Lloyd, father dead
             child was in Cleveland Orphan Asylum
adopters:    Lewis & Rebecca B Davis
new name:    Rosa Ann Davis
references:                      J 11: 142
date:        11 Nov 1870
    *

| | |
|---|---|
| adoptee: | Nannie Rockey Maines(?) aged 17Y on 20 Feb 1870 |
| parents: | dead, not named |
| adopters: | Mary B Campbell |
| new name: | Nannie Rockey Campbell |
| references: | J 11: 157 |
| date: | 5 Dec 1870 |

*

| | |
|---|---|
| adoptee: | Minnie Bumont(?) aged 3Y on 18 Dec 1870 |
| parents: | James D & Dora N Bumont, mother dead |
| adopters: | James N & Sarah K Brittingham |
| new name: | Minnie Brittingham |
| references: | J 11: 212 |
| date: | 28 Feb 1871 |

*

| | |
|---|---|
| adoptee: | William Fitzpatrick aged 16Y |
| parents: | Dorah Millay (or Mallay), father dead, not named |
| adopters: | Philip Millay of Columbus an unmarried man |
| new name: | William Millay |
| references: | J 11: 440 |
| date: | 30 Jan 1872 |

*

| | |
|---|---|
| adoptee: | Thurman Nickelson |
| parents: | Angelina Nickelson |
| adopters: | Daniel & Mahala Hagart |
| new name: | Daniel Thurman Hagart |
| references: | J 11: 502 |
| date: | 8 Apr 1872 |

*

| | |
|---|---|
| adoptee: | Edward Chapman aged 16M 4D on 16 June 1873 |
| parents: | Susan Chapman (not specifically identified as the mother, gave her consent) |
| adopters: | William H & Mary M Wing |
| new name: | Howard Everett Wing |
| references: | J 12: 295 |
| date: | 16 Jun 1873 |

*

| | |
|---|---|
| adoptee: | Ananias Newton Eaton |
| parents: | Sandy & Ann M Eaton, mother dead |
| adopters: | John R & Mary E Byrd |
| new name: | Ananias Newton Byrd |
| references: | J 12: 342 |
| date: | 1 Aug 1873 |

*

| | |
|---|---|
| adoptee: | Jennie Dewald aged 2M 8D on 21 Oct 1873 |
| parents: | John & Annie Dewald |
| adopters: | William J & Jennie Shotts |
| new name: | Effie Shotts |
| references: | J 12: 423 |
| date: | 21 Oct 1873 |

*

```
adoptee:        Leota Jordon aged 18M 7D on 22 Oct 1873
parents:        Jackson & Mary E Jordon
adopters:       John M & Mary L Jones
new name:       Nellie Leota (or Leotta) Jones
references:                     J 12: 425
date:           22 Oct 1873
         *
adoptee:        Mary Grace Browning aged 7M
parents:        Lucinda Browning
adopters:       Christopher & Lizzie Abblichon of Columbus
new name:       Mary Grace Abblichon
references:                     J 12: 438
date:           11 Nov 1873
         *
adoptee:        name unknown
parents:        unknown
adopters:       John & Camilla Hayes
new name:       Flora Elva Hayes
references:                     J 13: 280
date:           15 Dec 1874
         *
adoptee:        Harry Moore aged 3M on 18 Jan 1875
parents:        Margaret Moore, father dead
adopters:       Peter & Helena Vogt
new name:       Charles Vogt
references:                     J 13: 307
date:           8 Jan 1875
         *
adoptee:        Julia Rodgers aged 2Y 7M on 20 Jan 1876
parents:        Mary Rodgers
adopters:       John B & Mary A Skelton of FR Co
new name:       Julia Skelton
references:                     J 14: 114
date:           29 Jan 1876
         *
adoptee:        Bzotas Bryant (no age)
parents:        Mrs. Sarah M Bryant
adopters:       George W Allen
new name:       Bzotas Bright Allen
references:                     J 14: 133
date:           8 Feb 1876
         *
adoptee:        _____ Rover (male) aged 17D
parents:        Jacob K Rover, mother dead
adopters:       Frank H & Mamie Gervais of Columbus
new name:       Frank H Gervais
references:                     J 14: 148
date:           19 Feb 1876
         *
adoptee:        Georgina Catharine Buerstline aged 1Y 2M
parents:        John Wuest(?),     Elizabeth Buerstlein
adopters:       George & Catharine Buerstlein
new name:       no name change
```

references:                    J 14: 262
date:        19 June 1876
   *
adoptee:     male child aged 21W
parents:     none mentioned
adopters:    John & Anna D Kroger
new name:    Harry Albert Richard Kroger
references:                    J 14: 321
date:        8 Sep 1876
   *
adoptee:     female child aged 6M on 17 Feb 1877
parents:     unknown
adopters:    John & Josephine Walsh
new name:    Frances Bell Walsh
references:                    J 14: 466
date:        23 Feb 1877
   *
adoptee:     Ada Ann Filler aged 3Y
parents:     Eli Filler, mother dead
adopters:    John & Emma A Rinehart
new name:    Ada Ann Rinehart
references:                    J 14: 481
date:        10 Mar 1877
   *
adoptee:     Clarence L V Kring(?) (or Krug, Knirg, or
             King ?)  "Kring" in Civil Docket Index, #
parents:     Elmira Noble, father dead
adopters:    Oliver R Leffingwell, unmarried
new name:    no mention of a name change
references:                    J 14: 494
date:        20 Mar 1877
             # - aged 14Y on 6 June 1877
   *
adoptee:     Estella Nash aged 10Y Feb 1877 (no day)
parents:     none given
adopters:    Henry M & Lydia A Billings of FR Co
new name:    Estella Minnie Billings
references:                    J 14: 518
date:        7 Apr 1877
   *
adoptee:     Maud Lallaway aged 2Y on 23 Nov 1877
parents:     William Lallaway, mother "now named Cath-
             arine Leonard," divorced from father,
             mother had custody of the child
adopters:    John & Martha E James of Licking Co., OH
new name:    Eva Maud James
references:                    J 14: 564
date:        15 May 1877
   *
adoptee:     Carrie Jackson aged 14M
parents:     Patrick McGuire, Anna R Jackson
adopters:    Peter & Catharine M Darling
new name:    Carrie Darling

| | | |
|---|---|---|
| references: | | J 14: 566 |
| date: | 16 May 1877 | |

*

| | |
|---|---|
| adoptee: | Emma Heinig aged 4Y |
| parents: | Valentine Heinig, mother dead |
| adopters: | George Peter & Caroline Bader |
| new name: | Emma Bader |
| references: | J 15: 68 |
| date: | 10 Aug 1877 |

*

| | |
|---|---|
| adoptee: | Estella G. Fagenbush aged 7Y on 9 May 1877 |
| parents: | Samuel K. Fagenbush, mother dead |
| adopters: | Nathan & Almira M Croy |
| new name: | Estella G Croy |
| references: | J 15: 155 |
| date: | 6 Nov 1877 |

*

| | |
|---|---|
| adoptee: | Jennie Adams aged ca 9Y |
| parents: | none given, an orphan |
| adopters: | David & Mary D Lewis of FR Co |
| new name: | Jennie Adams Lewis |
| references: | J 15: 165 |
| date: | 22 Nov 1877 |

*

| | |
|---|---|
| adoptee: | Charles Eugene Elsey aged ca 18M |
| parents: | Samuel Elsey, mother dead |
| adopters: | Augustus & Ruth S Platt |
| new name: | Charles E Platt |
| references: | J 15: 341 |
| date: | 10 May 1878 |

*

| | |
|---|---|
| adoptee: | Polly Kenna aged under 5Y |
| parents: | unknown |
| adopters: | Isaac K & Mary J Hiltebrand (or Hildebrand) |
| new name: | Polly Hiltebrand |
| references: | J 15: 445 |
| date: | 2 Aug 1878 |

*

| | |
|---|---|
| adoptee: | Annie _____ "surname unknown" aged ca 3Y |
| parents: | unknown, an orphan |
| adopters: | John G & Rachel B Evans of FR Co |
| new name: | Gertrude P Evans |
| references: | J 16: 134 |
| date: | 7 Feb 1879 |

*

| | |
|---|---|
| adoptee: | Adaline H Richardson aged 9Y on 8 Nov 1879 |
| parents: | Aaron P & Sarah J Richardson; Sarah died on 20 Mar 1877 |
| adopters: | George A & Jennie Quimby of FR Co |
| new name: | Adaline H Quimby |
| references: | CR 10: 200     J 16: 196 |
| date: | 12 Mar 1879 |

*

adoptee:        Mable (or Mabel) Robinson aged 1Y on 10 Feb
                1880; ward of Cleveland Protestant Orphan
                Asylum
parents:        dead (not named)
adopters:       Henry W & Lucy A Spade of FR Co
new name:       Daisie Spade
references:     CR 10: 201        J 16: 262
date:           2 Apr 1879
                from J:  "...said child having previously
                been voluntarily surrendered by its parents
                to the Trustees of the Cleveland Protestant
                Orphan Asylum..."
        *

adoptee:        Bessie V Evans born 17 Oct 1875(?)
parents:        C D Evans of FR Co, mother dead
adopters:       George M & Esther L Adams of FR Co
new name:       Bessie Gertrude Adams
references:     CR 10: 296        J 16: 395
date:           28 May 1879
        *

adoptee:        _____ Cook (female) born 20 Aug 1879
                (child not given a first name)
parents:        Fanny Cook of Columbus
adopters:       Philipp & Mary Pitton of Columbus
new name:       Bertha Pitton
references:     CR 10: 512        J 17: 208
date:           9 Oct 1879
        *

adoptee:        Benjamin R Myers aged 6Y (7Y also used)
parents:        Ebenezer & Mary E Myers
adopters:       Herman C & Vialitta Pittelkow of Columbus
new name:       Benjamin R Pittelkow (or Pitkelow)
references:     CR 11: 37         J 17: 317, 321
date:           2 Dec 1879
                child was put in Home for the Friendless of
                Columbus by his parents at about age 2;
                child was a nephew of Vialitta (or Valitta
                or Valetta) Pittelkow
        *

adoptee:        Daisy Armor aged 1M on 11 Nov 1879
parents:        none mentioned
adopters:       Henry W & Lucy A Spade of Columbus
new name:       Bessie Edith Spade
references:     CR 11: 49         J 16: 253 & 17: 370
                child was a ward of the Cleveland Protestant
                Orphan Asylum
date:           23 Dec 1879
        *

adoptee:        Minerva Frances Evans born 21 Jan 1874
parents:        Columbus D Evans of FR Co, mother dead
adopters:       James Mickel (or Nickel) & wife Isabella
                C of FR Co
new name:       Minnie Frances Mickel (or Nickel)

references:    CR 11: 332        J 18: 94
date:          22 May 1880
        *
adoptee:       Adelia Meneley (or Menele) aged 8Y on 29
               Mar 1880
parents:       Amelia Meneley (or Menele)
adopters:      Herny & Amanda Smith of FR Co
new name:      Adelia A Smith
references:    CR 11: 499        J 18: 258
date:          21 Aug 1880
        *
adoptee:       Daisy May Pickering aged 2Y on 25 May 1881
               (aged 2Y on 28 May 1881 in J)
parents:       #S W & Jennie Pickering, mother dead
adopters:      Jefferson & Laura J Ferrel of FR Co
new name:      Daisy Pickering Ferrel
references:    CR 12: 90         J 19: 23
date:          12 Feb 1881
               #S W = Sylvanus Wood Pickering
        *
adoptee:       John Maloney aged 8M on 28 Apr 1881
parents:       Anna Maloney
adopters:      Peter & Lizzie Bates of FR Co
new name:      John Bates
references:    CR 12: 210        J 19: 168
date:          19 Apr 1881
        *
adoptee:       Albert John Smeltzer aged 5M on 26 Jun 1881
parents:       Charles & Minnie Smeltzer
adopters:      Charles & Christiana Lucks of FR Co
new name:      Charles Lucks
references:    CR 12: 410        J 19: 316
date:          2 Jul 1881
        *
adoptee:       Anne Ammonds aged 2Y on 13 Dec 1880
parents:       none mentioned, child was a ward of the
               Cleveland Protestant Orphan Asylum at age
               2Y 3M
adopters:      John & Eleanor H Cowgill of Camp Chase,
               FR Co
new name:      Mary Cowgill
references:    CR 12: 478        J 19: 376
date:          30 Jul 1881
        *
adoptee:       Edward Elijah Meacham aged 4Y on 27 Aug 1881
parents:       Elijah & Mary E Meacham, mother dead
adopters:      Thomas M & Rosetta M Kingry of Fr Co
new name:      Edward Elijah Kingry
references:    CR 12: 550        J 19: 441
date:          9 Sep 1881
        *
adoptee:       Effie Levisa Arnett aged 9Y on 29 Nov 1881
parents:       Ephraim & Martha Jane Arnett, both deceased

adopters:       Philip D & Mary V Patterson of FR Co
new name:       Effie Levisa (or Levitha) Patterson
references:     CR 13: 29          J 19: 456
date:           14 Sep 1881
        *

adoptee:        name unknown, aged 18M on 1 Sep 1881
parents:        unknown
adopters:       Henry F & Dora Gannon (or Ganon, Gannan)of
                FR Co
new name:       Mary Gannon (or Ganon)
references:     CR 13: 28          J 19: 481
                (erroneously listed as an estate in J)
date:           29 Sep 1881
        *

adoptee:        Harry Bradshaw Evans aged 1Y on 15 Aug 1881
parents:        Charles E Evans,  Jennie F. Benadum
adopters:       James B & Sarah D Evans of FR Co
new name:       no name change
references:     CR 13: 32          J 19: 526
date:           19 Oct 1881
        *

adoptee:        Eva May Redman aged 3Y on 3 Nov 1881
parents:        Frank Knowlton,  Anna Redman, father deceased
adopters:       Susan A Morehead, unmarried, of FR Co
new name:       Eva May Morehead
references:     CR 13: 31          J 19: 533
date:           24 Oct 1881
                see J 22: 84, 90, 97 for appeal to vacate
                adoption filed by Frederick Burnett
        *

adoptee:        Maud Pinney aged 9M on 9 Oct 1881
parents:        William Pinney,  Alice Spafford
adopters:       William & Amanda Sopher (or Sophar) of
                FR Co.
new name:       Maud Sopher
references:     CR 13: 126         J 20: 9
date:           23 Nov 1881
        *

adoptee:        William P Graff aged 2Y on 27 Mar 1882
parents:        Augustus B & Malissa Graff, mother dead
adopters:       Lemuel & Lavina Endley of FR Co
new name:       William Pore Endley
references:     CR 13: 173         J 20: 72
date:           17 Dec 1881
        *

adoptee:        Joseph Keller aged 2Y on 12 Aug 1882
parents:        Mary Keller
adopters:       Charles (or Carl) & Emilie Schmidt of FR Co
new name:       Joseph Schmidt
references:     CR 13: 169         J 20: 82
date:           22 Dec 1881
        *

```
adoptee:      Alta May Holland aged 1Y on 28 Dec 1882
parents:      Jane A Holland
adopters:     William & Margaretta Barrett of FR Co
new name:     Alta May Barrett
references:   CR 13: 198        J 20: 198
date:         31 Jan 1882
     *

adoptee:      Anna Kuebrich (or Kuebrick) aged 16Y on
              8 Oct 1881
parents:      August & Matilda Kuebrich, divorced, mother
              remarried to Charles Koehler (or Kohler),
              divorce took place in FR Co Court of Common
              Pleas
adopters:     Charles & Matilda Koehler (or Kohler) of FR
              Co
new name:     Anna Koehler
references:   CR 13: 371        J 20: 306
date:         14 Mar 1882
     *

adoptee:      William Kuebrich (or Kuebrick) aged 20Y
              on 15 Apr 1881
parents:      same as above
adopters:     same as above
new name:     William Koehler
references:   CR 13: 372        J 20: 306
date:         14 Mar 1882
     *

adoptee:      name unknown, aged 5Y on 5 Apr 1882
parents:      unknown, mother deceased
adopters:     Vincenz & Francis (or Franziska, Francisca)
              Buchholz (or Bucholz) of FR Co
new name:     John Buchholz
references:   CR 13: 379        J 20: 520, 522, 523
date:         25 May 1882  (see entry below)
     *

adoptee:      Ella Farrington alias Anna Buchholz aged
              12Y on 5 June 1882
parents:      Mr & Mrs Farrington, mother dead
adopters:     Vincenz & Francis Buchholz of FR Co
new name:     Anna (or Ella) Buchholz
references:   CR 13: 380        J 20: 519, 523
date:         25 May 1882 (see entry below)
     *

adoptee:      Sadie Farrington alias Lizzie Buchholz aged
              10Y on 16 Sep 1882
parents:      Mr & Mrs Farrington, mother dead
adopters:     Vincenz & Francis Buchholz of FR Co
new name:     Lizzie Buchholz
references:   CR 13: 382        J 20: 520, 524
date:         25 May 1882
     *

adoptee:      Joseph Orlando Remington aged 19Y on 20 Jan
              1882
```

parents:        Oscar & Almira Remington, mother remarried
                to Samuel B Gilbert, divorce implied between
                Oscar & Almira.
adopters:       Samuel B & Almira Gilbert of FR Co
new name:       Joseph Orlando Gilbert
references:     CR 13: 418        J 20: 559
date:           12 June 1882
      *

adoptee:        Annie Hutchins aged 1Y on 11 Apr 1882
parents:        none mentioned, at age 1Y child was bound
                to Cleveland Protestant Orphan Asylum
adopters:       John W & Annie E Randall of Columbus
new name:       Florence Mabel Randall
references:     CR 13: 548        J 21: 15
date:           7 Jul 1882
      *

adoptee:        Clarence Clare aged 8M on 19 Jul 1882
parents:        Charles & Clara Anne (or Annie) Clare,
                father died on 29 Mar 1881
adopters:       Brainerd D & Mary S Hills of FR Co
new name:       Clarence Clare Hills
references:     CR 13: 583        J 21: 48
date:           22 Jul 1882
      *

adoptee:        Willie Case aged 3M on 5 Nov 1882
parents:        Catharine Case
adopters:       John T & Mary Sager of FR Co
new name:       Charlie W Sager
references:     CR 14: 183        J 21: 307
date:           21 Nov 1882
      *

adoptee:        Joseph Radley aged 1Y on 1 Dec 1882
                a ward of the FR Co Children's Home
parents:        none mentioned
adopters:       James & Annie Winning of FR Co
new name:       Pearl Anderson Winning
references:     CR 14: 347        J 21: 542
date:           5 Mar 1883
      *

adoptee:        Edna H Hall aged 3Y on 22 Sep 1882
parents:        John & Angie Hall, father dead
adopters:       Lucius & Addie Walton of FR Co
new name:       Edna H Walton
references:     CR 14: 356        J 22: 12
date:           28 Mar 1883
      *

adoptee:        name unknown aged 9M on 3 May 1883
parents:        unknown, child has been in the custody
                of the McEwens since age 6W
adopters:       William S & Anna Carlisle McEwen of FR Co
new name:       Goldie McEwen
references:     CR 14: 500        J 22: 105
date:           12 May 1883
      *

adoptee:        William Anderson McDonald aged 3Y on 26 Feb
                1883
parents:        none mentioned, child was bound to the
                Cleveland Protestant Orphan Asylum at age 3Y
adopters:       John & Eleanor H Cowgill of Camp Chase, FR
                Co
new name:       William Harvey Cowgill
references:     CR 14: 499        J 22: 174
date:           9 Jun 1883
        *

adoptee:        Lavestie Edna Miner aged 2Y on 25 Dec 1882
parents:        Samuel L & Mary Ann Miner, father died on
                10 Jan 1881, a resident of Sharon Twp, FR Co
adopters:       Thomas M & Rosetta M Kingry of FR Co
new name:       Lavestie Edna Kingry
references:     CR 15: 13         J 22: 310
date:           13 Aug 1883
        *

adoptee:        Minnie Johnston aged 5Y on 18 Nov 1882
parents:        unknown, Minnie was previously adopted in
                Champaign Co., OH, by Alexander & Emily
                Johnston, Alexander died 6 May 1883
adopters:       Philip & Fredericka Ulrich (or Uhrich) of Fr
                Co
new name:       Minnie Ulrich (or Uhrich)
references:     CR 15: 117        J 22: 360
date:           4 Sep 1883
        *

adoptee:        Myrtle (or Myrdia) Gardner (or Garner)
                aged 5Y on 30 Aug 1883
parents:        William H & Bell(e) Garner, mother dead
                child was a ward of the FR Co. Children's
                Home
adopters:       David & Hannah L Altman of FR Co
new name:       Myrtle Altman
references:     CR 15: 316        J 22: 533
date:           20 Nov 1883
        *

adoptee:        Myrtie Bell aged 2Y on 6 Mar 1883
parents:        Cyrus C & Nancy Bell
adopters:       Andrew O & Rosetta (or Rozeta) M Bonnett
                of FR Co
new name:       Myrtie Bonnett
references:     CR 15: 402        J 23: 22,23
date:           21 Dec 1883
        *

adoptee:        Charles Allen aged 15M on 26 Feb 1884
parents:        Catharine Allen
adopters:       Joseph & Laura A Gibbard of FR Co
new name:       Charles Allen Gibbard
references:     CR 15: 492        J 23: 158
date:           19 Feb 1884
        *

adoptee:        Stella Belle _____ (surname unknown)
                aged 4Y on 5 Jan 1884
parents:        unknown
adopters:       Frank & Isabella Collins of FR Co
new name:       Stella Belle Collins
references:     CR 16: 97      J 23: 412
date:           12 Jun 1884
        *

adoptee:        Vevie Conway aged 1Y on 3 Sep 1884
parents:        Lou Conway (mother)
adopters:       Peter & Sarah Potter of FR Co
new name:       Janetta Potter
references:     CR 16: 159     J 23: 432
date:           26 June 1884
        *

adoptee:        name unknown, aged 6M on 19 Jun 1884
                (or 17 June according to J entry)
parents:        unknown
adopters:       Lawrence (or Loren) & Sarah E Winstaffer
                of FR Co
new name:       Thomas Williard Winstaffer
references:     CR 16: 158     J 23: 435
date:           27 Jun 1884
        *

adoptee:        Charles Newton Epley aged 11Y on 6 Oct
                1884
parents:        William A & Adaline (or Angeline) Epley
                mother dead
adopters:       Robert & Angeline Patterson of FR Co
new name:       Charles Epley Patterson
references:     CR 16: 242     J 23: 524
date:           2 Aug 1884
        *

adoptee:        Myrtle Gainer (or Gaines ?) aged 2Y on
                9 Oct 1884
parents:        _____ Cook (father), Mollie Gainer (or
                Gaines ?)-mother (dead)
adopters:       George F & Katharina Constans of Fr Co
new name:       Gracie Katie Constans
references:     CR 561         J 24: 266
date:           11 Dec 1884
        *

adoptee:        Eliza Ruth Palmer aged 5Y on 12 Jul 1885
parents:        William Francis (middle name) & Mary
                Palmer,(father dead), see also next entry
adopters:       James R & Eliza Jane Ashbaugh of FR Co
new name:       Eliza Ruth Ashbaugh
references:     CR 16: 558     J 24: 304
date:           29 Dec 1884
        *

adoptee:        Lucy Elizabeth Palmer aged 6Y on 22 Feb
                1885
parents:        same as above - father died on 20 Feb 1884

```
adopters:       Charles & Sarah Hafer of FR Co
new name:       Lucy Elizabeth Hafer
references:     CR 16: 559        J 24: 304
date:           29 Dec 1884
        *
adoptee:        Olive Gertrude Thompson aged 2Y on 24 Jan
                1885
parents:        David J & Jennette S Thompson, father dead
adopters:       George Frederick (middle name) & Emma
                Brodbeck of FR Co
new name:       Olive Gertrude  Brodbeck
references:     CR 17: 79         J 24: 314
date:           2 Jan 1885
        *
adoptee:        Ida Shipe aged 7Y on 6 Apr 1884 (or 1885
                according to J entry)
parents:        Lydia Shipe, a widow; father died 16 July
                1883 (not named) - _____ Shipe.
adopters:       S D & Mary Sweny of FR Co
new name:       Ida Sweny
references:     CR 17: 83         J 24: 390
date:           20 Jan 1885
        *
adoptee:        Fredie Spencer aged 5Y on _____ 1884
                a ward of the FR Co Children's Home
parents:        unknown
adopters:       Edward & Rosetta Steffens (or Steffin)
                of FR Co
new name:       Fredie Steffens (or Steffin)
references:     CR 17: 107        J 24: 490
date:           13 Feb 1885
        *
adoptee:        William Mueller aged ca 3½Y on 18 Feb
                1885
parents:        Louise Mueller
adopters:       Henry & Mary Meinson (or Meinsen) of FR Co
new name:       William H Meinson (or Meinsen)
references:     CR 17: 105        J 24: 496, 497
date:           18 Feb 1885
        *
adoptee:        Wallace H L Hommedien (or Hommedian,
                Hommendien) aged 5Y on 9 Mar 1885 and
                Ethel L Hommedien aged 2Y on 12 Aug 1885
parents:        Fred L & Bell L Hommedien, mother dead
adopters:       Amos & Orilla V Graham of Truro Twp, FR Co
new name:
references:     CR 17: 143        J 24: 547
date:           no date given in CR [1885]
        *
adoptee:        Rodney Crain aged 2Y on 23 Dec 1885
parents:        A K(?) & Cora Crain, mother dead
adopters:       James E & Anna Martin(?) of FR Co
new name:       Edward Rodney Martin
```

```
references:                    J 25: 152
date:        29 May 1885 (father possibly Abraham K Crane)
    *
adoptee:     Jennie Bell Walcutt (or Wolcutt, Wolcott)
             aged 15Y on 23 Nov 1885
parents:     Rheal & Kate Wolcott (or Wolcutt), both
             dead
adopters:    DeWitt & Isabel Rockwell of FR Co
new name:    Jennie Bell Rockwell
references:  CR 17: 589        J 26: 84
date:        24 Nov 1885
    *
adoptee:     Dolly Sands
parents:     Joseph & Harriet Sands
adopters:    Adam & Clara Kirschner
new name:
references:                    J 26: 9
date:        16 Dec 1885
             "Cause dismissed - proceedings terminated"
             [adoption apparently never took place]
    *
adoptee:     Emma F Burton aged 16Y on 28 Jan 1885
parents:     Harriet S. Simpson "nee Burton"
adopters:    Charles E & Harriet Simpson of FR Co
new name:    Emma F Simpson
references:  CR 18: 201        J 26: 20
date:        17 Dec 1885  (see also entry below)
    *
adoptee:     Edmund Smith aged 4Y on 6 Oct 1885
parents:     Rush & Jennie V Smith, Jennie died about
             2 years ago
adopters:    Charles E & Harriet S Simpson of FR Co
new name:    Edmund Simpson
references:  CR 18: 202        J 26: 19
date:        17 Dec 1885
    *
adoptee:     Anna Mary Dickerson aged 6Y on 18 June 1886
parents:     William W & Jessie Dickerson, Jessie was
             the stepmother to Anna
adopters:    William W Hull (or Hall ?), a widower of
             FR Co
new name:    Anna Mary Hull (or Hall ?)
references:                    J 26: 322
date:        12 Apr 1886
    *
adoptee:     George W Berg aged 8W on 3 May 1886
parents:     Martha Berg
adopters:    William & Ann Baily of FR Co
new name:    George W Baily
references:                    J 26: 383
date:        4 May 1886
    *
```

adoptee:      Bessie Maria McMillen (or McMellen) aged
              10Y on 27 Nov 1885
parents:      Solomon H(?) & Charlotte A McMillen
adopters:     John F & Charlotte A Herman of FR Co
new name:     Bessie Maria McMellen Herman
references:                   J 27: 78
date:         8 Sep 1886
     *

adoptee:      William Achuff aged 20Y on 6 Jan 1887
parents:      Lois Field(s), a widow, formerly Lois
              Achuff; father - William Achuff, dead
adopters:     John & Almenia Fell of FR Co
new name:     William A Fell
references:                   J 27: 544
date:         17 Feb 1887
     *

adoptee:      Maggie Throckmorton aged 3Y on 10 Aug
              1887
parents:      _____ & Mary Throckmorton, father's
              first name not known, his surname was
              Throckmorton
adopters:     David & Emma L Fittro of FR Co
new name:     Mary Fittro
references:                   J 28: 236, 244
date:         9 May 1887
     *

adoptee:      Ervin Horch aged 2Y on 13 Jan 1887
parents:      Howel & Mary Horch
adopters:     Charles I(?) & Mary Ann Benns of FR Co
new name:     Ervin Benns
references:                   J 28: 349
date:         15 June 1887
     *

adoptee:      Bridget Elizabeth Cody aged 9Y on 27 Feb
              1887
parents:      Michael & Elizabeth Cody
adopters:     John E & Mary Doyle of FR Co
new name:     Elizabeth Doyle
references:                   J 28: 358
date:         22 June 1887
     *

adoptee:      Paul Bethge aged 3Y on 1887 (no day/mo)
parents:      Alfred Beebe
adopters:     Joseph Bernard (middle name) & Elizabeth
              W Zettler of FR Co
new name:     Paul Bethge Zettler
references:                   J 29: 26, 27
date:         20 Sep 1887
     *

adoptee:      Frederick Rickenbacher aged 6Y on 3 Mar
              1881 (should possibly read 1887 ?)
parents:      John Rickenbacher, Mary Parker
              child was a ward of the FR Co Children's

|             |                                                             |
|-------------|-------------------------------------------------------------|
|             | Home                                                        |
| adopters:   | Jerome & Louisa (or Laura) Schmeltz of FR Co                |
| new name:   | Fred Schmeltz                                               |
| references: | J 29: 82                                                    |
| date:       | 15 Oct 1887                                                 |

*

| adoptee:    | name unknown (no age given)                                 |
|-------------|-------------------------------------------------------------|
| parents:    | unknown                                                      |
| adopters:   | Amos W & Samantha C Petticord of FR Co                      |
| new name:   | Dora Mabel Petticord                                        |
| references: | J 29: 181                                                   |
| date:       | 19 Nov 1887                                                 |

*

| adoptee:    | Minnie F Watson aged 4Y on 21 Dec 1887                      |
|-------------|-------------------------------------------------------------|
| parents:    | Samuel W & Francis J(?) Watson                              |
| adopters:   | Forrest & Sarah M Allen of FR Co                           |
| new name:   | name to remain the same                                    |
| references: | J 29: 222                                                   |
| date:       | 3 Dec 1887                                                  |

*

| adoptee:    | John H Walley aged 10Y on 20 Jan 1888                      |
|-------------|-------------------------------------------------------------|
| parents:    | John & Jane Walley, father dead                            |
| adopters:   | S D & Mary Sweeney of FR Co                                |
| new name:   | name to remain the same                                    |
| references: | J 29: 560                                                   |
| date:       | 9 Mar 1888                                                  |

*

| adoptee:    | Beatrice Kiel aged 7W on 31 Mar 1888                       |
|-------------|-------------------------------------------------------------|
| parents:    | Anna Kiel                                                    |
| adopters:   | Jerry & Eliza Grimes of FR Co                              |
| new name:   | Beatrice Grimes                                            |
| references: | J 30: 38                                                    |
| date:       | 29 Mar 1888                                                 |

*

| adoptee:    | Earl Leonard aged 4Y on 4 Jun 1888                         |
|-------------|-------------------------------------------------------------|
| parents:    | mother dead                                                  |
| adopters:   | Eli D & Mary E Minor (or Miner) of FR Co                   |
| new name:   | Earl D Minor (or Miner)                                    |
| references: | J 30: 56                                                    |
| date:       | 5 Apr 1888                                                  |

*

| adoptee:    | Mary Hartel aged 3Y on 12 Mar 1888                         |
|-------------|-------------------------------------------------------------|
| parents:    | unknown                                                      |
| adopters:   | Kansas & Hattie Baughman of FR Co                          |
| new name:   | Bertha May Baughman                                        |
| references: | J 30: 101                                                   |
| date:       | 19 Apr 1888                                                 |
|             | child was a ward of the FR Co Children's Home              |

*

| adoptee:    | Francis Nicholas Lang aged 10W on 13 May 1888             |
|-------------|-------------------------------------------------------------|

| | |
|---|---|
| parents: | Martin & Annie Lang |
| adopters: | Nicholas & Margaret Roche of FR Co |
| new name: | Francis Nicholas Roche |
| references: | J 30: 205 |
| date: | 23 May 1888 |

\*

| | |
|---|---|
| adoptee: | Clara Belle Dunham aged 2Y on 2 Apr 1888 |
| parents: | William P Dunham |
| adopters: | John C & May Price of FR Co |
| new name: | Clara Belle Price |
| references: | J 30: 260 |
| date: | 14 Jun 1888 |

\*

| | |
|---|---|
| adoptee: | Robert Tracey aged 3M 18D, born on 23 Mar 1888 |
| parents: | James Ruckman, Carrie Tracey |
| adopters: | Robert & Irene Joiner of FR Co |
| new name: | Robert Huston Joiner |
| references: | J 30: 323 |
| date: | 11 Jul 1888 |

\*

| | |
|---|---|
| adoptee: | Harry Clayton aged 8M on 22 Jul 1888 |
| parents: | unknown, child was a ward of the FR Co Children's Home |
| adopters: | Elisha & Emma Brown of Emma Brown |
| new name: | Harry Clayton Brown |
| references: | J 30: 367 |
| date: | 28 Jul 1888 |

\*

| | |
|---|---|
| adoptee: | Francisca Gatterdam aged 14Y on 6 Dec 1888 |
| parents: | Casper & Catharine Gatterdam, divorced, Casper had legal custody of the child |
| adopters: | Augustus A & Elizabeth A Burkley of FR Co |
| new name: | no name change mentioned |
| references: | J 31: 158 |
| date: | 5 Dec 1888 |

\*

| | |
|---|---|
| adoptee: | Veloy Pearl Bailey aged 9Y on 9 Feb 1889 |
| parents: | Martin L & Lizzie J Bailey |
| adopters: | James M & Ella Eisenhart of FR Co |
| new name: | Veloy Pearl Eisenhart |
| references: | J 31: 420 |
| date: | 25 Feb 1889 |

\*

| | |
|---|---|
| adoptee: | Thomas Hall aged 10Y on 30 Jun 1889 |
| parents: | Judgie Hall, Julia Elizabeth Clark, formerly Julia Elizabeth Sharp |
| adopters: | Edward & Alice Getreu (or Getrue) of FR Co |
| new name: | Thomas Getreu (or Getrue) |
| references: | J 31: 540 |
| date: | 26 Mar 1889 |

\*

adoptee:     Blanch Alma Arnold aged 15Y on 31 May 1890
parents:     Charles & Saddie A Arnold
adopters:    Joseph W & Sadie A Brooks, formerly Sadie
             A Arnold, of FR Co
new name:    Blanch Brooks
references:                  J 32: 254
date:        17 Jun 1889
       *

adoptee:     Blanche Sprague aged 12Y on 13 Aug 1889
parents:     Oscar & Ella F Sprague
adopters:    Cornelius & Catharine Perdue of FR Co
new name:    Blanche Perdue
references:                  J 32: 474
date:        28 Aug 1889
       *

adoptee:     Saddie Curley aged 4Y on 25 Jun 1889
parents:     _____ & Katie (or Kate) Curley, first
             name of Mr. Curley not given
adopters:    Charles R & Mary A Meredith of FR Co
new name:    Saddie Meredith
references:                  J 33: 15
date:        21 Oct 1889
       *

adoptee:     James Stinson, Jr aged 13Y on 22 Nov 1889
parents:     James & Kate Stinson, mother dead
adopters:    Joseph & Mollie Messmer of FR Co
new name:    James Messmer
references:                  J 33: 183
date:        20 Dec 1889
       *

adoptee:     Henrietta Redman aged 1Y on 4 Aug 1889
parents:     Mary E Redman, deceased; a Julia Redman
             served as "next friend" of the child in
             this adoption
adopters:    John T & Belle Redman of FR Co
new name:    no name change
references:                  J 33: 532
date:        15 Apr 1890
       *

adoptee:     _____ McNally (no first name given)
             aged 2M on 15 Apr 1890
parents:     Alice McNally
adopters:    Valentine & Elizabeth T Loewer of FR Co
new name:    Mabel Elizabeth Loewer
references:                  J 34: 5
date:        1 May 1890
       *

adoptee:     Zoe (or Joe ?) Airs (or Avis ?) Jackson
             aged 6Y on 20 Sep 1890
parents:     James Y & Laura B Jackson
adopters:    James H & Sarah A Shreeves
new name:    Joe Avis(?) Shreeves
references:                  J 34: 304

date:          5 Sep 1890
   *
adoptee:       Frank Stager aged 1Y on 20 Dec 1890
parents:       Caroline Stager
adopters:      Peter & Hattie Jones of FR Co
new name:      Frank Jones
references:                        J 34: 369
date:          29 Sep 1890
   *
adoptee:       George Busch aged 6M
parents:       George & Matilda Busch
adopters:      John Anton (middle name) & Josette (or
               Jaretta) Vath of FR Co
new name:      John Anton Vath
references:                        J 34: 439
date:          23 Oct 1890
   *
adoptee:       Mabel Eliza Johnston aged 8W on 14 Nov
               1890
parents:       Dora Johnston
adopters:      Samuel & Kate Peterman of FR Co
new name:      Mabel Eliza Peterman
references:                        J 34: 496
date:          14 Nov 1890
   *
adoptee:       May Sinns (or Simms ?) aged 6Y on 15 Dec
               1890
parents:       _____ Sinns (or Simms ?), Margaret
               Mahoney
adopters:      Drusius B & Nellie A Read of FR Co
new name:      Mena(?) L Read
references:                        J 34: 552
date:          1 Dec 1890
   *
adoptee:       Mary Leila Woodside aged 1Y on 2 Jul 1890
parents:       Stella Woodside
adopters:      William & Amelia Wiggins of FR Co
new name:      Mary Leila Wiggins
references:                        J 34: 568
date:          6 Dec 1890
   *
adoptee:       Mary Florence _____ (surname unknown)
               aged 1Y on 17 Jan 1892
parents:       unknown
adopters:      Patrick & Julia Donahue of FR Co
new name:      Mary Florence Donahue
references:    CR 25: 572        J 36: 211
date:          12 Jan 1891
   *
adoptee:       Amelia Henneke(r) aged 6Y on 22 Oct 1890
parents:       Henry & Kate Henneke, mother dead
adopters:      Detrick & Barbara Henneke of Columbus
new name:

references:          CR 26: 77          J 35: 191, 210, 215
date:                12 Feb 1891
                     Henry Henneke refused to surrender Amelia
                     to Detrick & Barbara Henneke; adoption was
                     revoked on 18 Feb 1891; Amelia remained
                     with Henry.

        *

adoptee:             Mabel Cadwallader (real name unknown),
                     aged 9Y on 22 Feb 1891 (23 Feb also used)
parents:             unknown
adopters:            Sarah Cadwallader of FR Co
new name:
references:          CR 26: 123         J 35: 273
date:                7 Mar 1891

        *

adoptee:             William Swarbrick aged 21 on 12 Oct 1891
parents:             Richard & Alice Jane Swarbrick
adopters:            Alexander Winward, a widower, of FR Co
new name:            William Swarbrick Winward
references:          CR 26: 125         J 35: 310, 362
date:                1 April 1891 (18 Oct 1890)
                     a John Thos. Swarbrick also served as a
                     witness

        *

adoptee:             John Karnes aged 3Y on 13 May 1891
parents:             John F & Odelia Karnes, mother dead
adopters:            John E & Ella Price of FR Co
new name:            John Karnes Price
references:          CR 25: 442         J 35: 566
date:                26 May 1891

        *

adoptee:             Geneva Adkins aged 6Y on 26 (or 20) June
                     1892
parents:             John & Nannie Adkins
adopters:            James L & Mattie Faucitt (or Faucett,
                     Fausitt) of FR Co
new name:            Geneva Faucett
references:          CR 26: 135         J 36: 233
date:                22 Aug 1891

        *

adoptee:             Fay Alice Goodin aged 9Y on 26 Sep 1892
parents:             James & Catharine Goodin
adopters:            Sisters of the Good Shepherd of FR Co.
                     by Sister Mary Germain(e)
new name:            no name change
references:          CR 26: 249         J 36: 367
date:                6 Oct 1891

        *

adoptee:             Maud(e) May Green aged 9Y on 22 Dec 1892
parents:             Alexander & Ruth Green, father dead
adopters:            Francis Martier (or Moitier, Mortner ?)
new name:            no name change
references:          CR 26: 251         J 36: 367

| | |
|---|---|
| date: | 6 oct 1891 |
| * | |
| adoptee: | _____ Blazer (male) aged 1Y on 26 Oct 1892 (no first name given) |
| parents: | Mrs. I(?) Blazer |
| adopters: | John Frank (middle name) & Louisa Ranney (or Raney) of FR Co |
| new name: | Oliver Ranney (or Raney) |
| references: | CR 26: 382        J 36: 514 |
| date: | 24 Nov 1891 |
| * | |
| adoptee: | Gertrude M Mealheim (or Malheim, Mealhiem, Mealhien) aged 1Y on 26 Jun 1892 |
| parents: | Clara Mealheim (or Mealhiem) |
| adopters: | George W & Jennie M Stine of FR Co |
| new name: | Cora Margaretta Stine |
| references: | CR 26: 452        J 36: 547 |
| date: | 3 Dec 1891 |
| * | |
| adoptee: | Nanie (or Manie, Minnie) Maud Parsons aged 11Y on 6 (or 1st) Jan 1892 (this child was also referred to as Maude or Marie Alice Parsons) |
| parents: | Alice (or Allice) Lowers (or Lowens ?) |
| adopters: | Sisters of the Good Shepherd of FR Co Mother Teresa; Sister Mary Angela (or Agnes) also signed |
| new name: | no name change |
| references: | CR 26: 450        J 36: 557 |
| date: | 8 Dec 1891 |
| | father of the child was dead |
| * | |
| adoptee: | Mary Ethel Smith aged 6Y on 30 May 1892 |
| parents: | George B & Lucy M Smith, mother dead |
| adopters: | William & Amanda Spangler of FR Co |
| new name: | Mary Ethel Spangler |
| references: | CR 26: 474        J 36: 560 |
| date: | 8 Dec 1891 |
| | a George D Spangler and a Fillmore Spangler served as witnesses |
| * | |
| adoptee: | Maribel Knoderer aged 8Y on 8 Sep 1892 |
| parents: | William A & Clara Belle Knoderer, Clara remarried to Columbus D Saviers |
| adopters: | Columbus D & Clara Belle Saviers |
| new name: | Maribel Phyllis Saviers |
| references: | CR 27: 75        J 37: 146 |
| date: | 8 Feb 1892 |
| * | |
| adoptee: | name unknown, aged 2Y on 19 Oct 1893 |
| parents: | unknown |
| adopters: | Andrew & Minnie J Sendelbach of FR Co |
| new name: | Mary Josephine Sendelbach |

```
references:     CR 27: 77        J 37: 275
date:           11 Mar 1892
     *
adoptee:        Helen Kennedy aged 6Y on 26 Nov 1892
parents:        Mary Kennedy
adopters:       Solomon S & Eliza N Moore of FR Co
new name:       Helen Moore
references:     CR 27: 100       J 37: 343
date:           28 Mar 1892
     *
adoptee:        Percy Scott aged 9Y on 6 Jan 1893
parents:        William & Bertha Scott, both dead
adopters:       Louisa (or Louise) Stafford, a widow,
                of FR Co
new name:       Percy Scott Stafford
references:     CR 27: 102       J 37: 356
date:           31 Mar 1892
     *
adoptee:        Bessie Adeline Ryan aged 2Y on 8 Oct 1892
parents:        Jane Ryan, father dead
adopters:       Sandusky (or Samuel) & Emma Redman
                of FR Co
new name:       Bessie Adeline Redman
references:     CR 27: 106       J 37: 448
date:           23 Apr 1892
     *
adoptee:        William _____ (last name unknown)
                aged 1Y on 2 Dec 1892
parents:        unknown
adopters:       William & Alice F Eisel of FR Co
new name:       William Eiser
references:     CR 27: 104       J 37: 533
date:           14 May 1892
     *
adoptee:        Mary Caldwell aged 10Y on 10 (or 11) Oct
                1891 and Mable Caldwell aged 6Y on 14 Apr
                1891
parents:        John & Ida Caldwell, father dead
adopters:       Sisters of the Good Shepherd of FR Co
                Sister M Agnes
new name:       none mentioned
references:     CR 27: 113       J 38: 6
date:           6 Jun 1892
     *
adoptee:        Mary Ingalls aged 7Y on _____ 1892
                (no day/mo given)
parents:        Francis Ingalls (or Ingal), female
adopters:       Sisters of the Good Shepherd of FR Co
                Sister M Angeline (or Angela)
new name:       none mentioned
references:     CR 27: 111       J 38: 25
date:           10 Jun 1892
     *
```

| adoptee: | name unknown, born on 10 June 1892 |
| parents: | unknown |
| adopters: | J W & Mrs. Beathard (no first name given for wife) of FR Co |
| new name: | John Rosal Beathard |
| references: | CR 28: 11        J 38: 88 |
| date: | 30 June 1892 |

*

| adoptee: | Grace Cord aged 7Y on 16 Mar 1893 |
| parents: | _____ Cord (female) |
| adopters: | Joseph D & Rosa B Evans of FR Co |
| new name: | Grace Evans |
| references: | CR 28: 23        J 38: 313 |
| date: | 17 Sep 1892 |

*

| adoptee: | Mary Rebecca Kile aged 7Y on 7 Feb 1892 |
| parents: | William Kile,  Clara Geary (or Gerry) |
| adopters: | John E & Ianthus L Evans |
| new name: | Mary Rebecca Evans |
| references: | CR 28: 7        J 38: 222 |
| date: | 20 Aug 1892 |

*

| adoptee: | Lillie Bolen, born 7 Feb 1892 |
| parents: | Urie Bolen (mother) |
| adopters: | Frank & Jennie Williams of FR Co |
| new name: | Lillie Williams |
| references: | CR 28: 9        J 38: 238 |
| date: | 26 Aug 1892 |

*

| adoptee: | May Hyle aged 6Y on 13 Dec 1891 |
| parents: | George Jefferson (middle name) & Phillip-anna Hyle, mother dead |
| adopters: | James & Elizabeth Lynas of FR Co |
| new name: | May Hyle Lynas |
| references: | CR 28: 25        J 38: 260 |
| date: | 1 Sep 1892 |

*

| adoptee: | Etta (or Ettie) Foster aged 7Y and Elsy (or Elsie) Foster aged 4Y |
| parents: | Wilson & Lucy Foster |
| adopters: | Charlotte Kelley (or Kelly), a widow of FR Co |
| new name: | |
| references: | CR 28: 29        J 38: 304 |
| date: | 14 Sep 1892 |

*

| adoptee: | Maria Phillips aged 12Y on 8 Jun 1892 & Olive (or Oliver) Phillips aged 3Y on 29 Mar 1892 |
| parents: | Jesse & Anna L Phillips |
| adopters: | Sisters of the Good Shepherd of FR Co Sister Angela |
| new name: | |

```
references:    CR 28: 27          J 38: 421
date:          18 Oct 1892
     *
adoptee:       Hellie Hazel Sheaf aged 3Y on 1 Nov 1892
parents:       George Colbach(?),   Emma E Sheaf
adopters:      John L & Jennie C Martin of FR Co
new name:      Nellie Hazel Martin
references:    CR 28: 252         J 38: 437
date:          24 Oct 1892
     *
adoptee:       Chester Joyce aged 3Y on 12 Mar 1893
               (12 Mar 1892 also used)
parents:       Charles M & Mary F Joyce, mother dead
adopters:      Henry H & Amanda M Sibley of FR Co
new name:      Chester Sibley
references:    CR 28: 253         J 38: 470
date:          2 Nov 1892
     *
adoptee:       Harrold Moehn aged 3Y on 23 Sep 1893
parents:       Abraham & Emma Moehn (or Moehm)
adopters:      John & Dela Shrock of FR Co
new name:      George Harrold Shrock
references:    CR 28: 255         J 38: 478
date:          5 Nov 1892
     *
adoptee:       Walter Brown aged 19Y on 6 Mar 1893
parents:       John Brown, dead, & Mrs  Hattie L Hyne,
               mother remarried to George D Hyne
adopters:      Addison Blair (or Blain ?), a widower,
               of FR Co
new name:      Walter Blair (or Blain ?)
references:    CR 28: 75          J 38: 536
date:          25 Nov 1892
     *
adoptee:       Blanche Cockrell aged 7Y on 12 Apr 1893
parents:       Jasper & Rachall (or Rachal, Rachel)
               Cockeral (or Cockerall, Cockrell)
adopters:      Sisters of the Good Shepherd of FR Co
               Sister Angela
new name:      a name change was implied, but none given
references:    CR 28: 77          J 38: 537
date:          25 Nov 1892
     *
adoptee:       Frank Roedelsberger aged 4Y on 30 May 1893
parents:       Peter & Lizzie Roedelsberger, mother dead
adopters:      Paulus & Margaretha Barbara Thaler of FR
               Co
new name:      no name change
references:    CR 28: 250         J 38: 575
date:          7 Dec 1892
     *
```

adoptee:        Ada Florence Devan aged 13Y and
                Victoria Bell Devan aged 10Y
parents:        William & Anna (or Annie) Devan, father
                dead
adopters:       Sisters of the Good Shepherd of FR Co
                Sister M Agness
new name:
references:     CR 28: 256      J 39: 23
date:           20 Dec 1892
    *
adoptee:        Mable Coonts aged 13Y on 19 Jan 1893
parents:        William H & Martha A Coonts (or Coontz),
                mother dead; William H  Huber stepfather
                of said child
adopters:       Mary E Carpenter, not married, of FR Co
new name:       Mable Carpenter
references:     CR 28: 508      J 39: 176
date:           6 Feb 1893
    *
adoptee:        _____ White (no first name) aged 3M on
                9 Apr 1893
parents:        Mabel White
adopters:       Frank E & Ida J Wylie of FR Co
new name:       Frank M Wylie
references:     CR 29: 94       J 39: 355
date:           30 Mar 1893
    *
adoptee:        _____ Fenstermaker (no first name)
                born 31 Jan 1893
parents:        Lulu Fenstermaker
adopters:       John Adolf (first name) & Armie(?) Hesse
                of FR Co
new name:       Lester Adolf Hesse
references:     CR 29: 105      J 39: 401
date:           13 Apr 1893
                an F M Fenstermaker served as a witness
    *
adoptee:        _____ Kinser (no first name) born 24
                Mar 1893
parents:        Anna Kinser
adopters:       John Wallace (middle name) & Rosey Leander
                (or Fender) Scott of FR Co
new name:       Harry Scott
references:     CR 27: 436      J 40: 9
date:           31 May 1893
                a Mary J Kinser served as a witness
    *
adoptee:        Helen Litchford aged 2Y on 25 Jun 1894
parents:        Stella A Litchford of Columbus
adopters:       John W & Ellen Jackson of Columbus
new name:       Helen Jackson
references:     CR 31: 384      J 43: 225
date:           1 Jun 1893
    *

| | |
|---|---|
| adoptee: | name unknown, aged 10M on 6 Jan 1893 |
| parents: | unknown |
| adopters: | Hugh B & Bell D Fleming of FR Co |
| new name: | Nellie Marie Fleming |
| references: | CR 28: 249      J 39: 113 |
| date: | 18 June 1893 |

\*

| | |
|---|---|
| adoptee: | Jennie Madden aged 2Y on 22 May 1893 |
| parents: | John & Jennie Madden, father dead |
| adopters: | Joseph Edwin (middle name) & Emma Florence Harris of FR Co |
| new name: | Florence Louis Harris |
| references: | CR 27: 434      J 40: 203 this adoption was later reversed, see J 60: 516 |
| date: | 3 Aug 1893 |

\*

| | |
|---|---|
| adoptee: | Grace Beavers aged 6Y on 15 Feb 1893 |
| parents: | Nelson & Alice Beavers, mother dead |
| adopters: | William P & Martha Jane Bard of FR Co |
| new name: | Grace Bard |
| references: | CR 27: 432      J 40: 242 |
| date: | 16 Aug 1893 |

\*

| | |
|---|---|
| adoptee: | Fannie Mary Butt aged 18Y on 7 (or 9?) Apr 1893 |
| parents: | Samuel & Margaret Butt |
| adopters: | Mary Rockwell of FR Co |
| new name: | Fannie Mary Rockwell |
| references: | CR 29: 418      J 40: 267 |
| date: | 25 Aug 1893 a Dewitt Rockwell served as a witness |

\*

| | |
|---|---|
| adoptee: | Maud Mitchell aged 9M on 9 Nov 1891 |
| parents: | Jennie Mitchell |
| adopters: | Charley & Sophia Gunkle of FR Co |
| new name: | Bertha Gunkle |
| references: | CR 29: 419      J 40: 284 |
| date: | 31 Aug 1893 |

\*

| | |
|---|---|
| adoptee: | _____ Kent (no first name) aged 6W on 30 Sep 1893 |
| parents: | "_____ Kent and _____" |
| adopters: | John L & Ellen Nienkirchen of FR Co |
| new name: | Clarence Louis Nienkirchen |
| references: | CR 29: 499      J 40: 402 |
| date: | 10 Oct 1893 |

\*

| | |
|---|---|
| adoptee: | Emma Wright aged 7Y on 7 Jul 1893 |
| parents: | Henry & Lydia Wright |
| adopters: | Samuel H & Louisa Gray of FR Co |
| new name: | Emma Gray |
| references: | CR 29: 571      J 40: 456 |

date:            27 Oct 1893
    *
adoptee:         Anna Judson aged 2M on 18 Nov 1893
parents:         Ora Judson (mother)
adopters:        Fred & Johanna Hischke of FR Co
new name:        Anna Greta Hischke
references:      CR 30: 86        J 40: 499
date:            14 Nov 1893
    *
adoptee:         Alice Delaney aged 7Y on 15 May 1893
parents:         Ed & Mary Delaney, mother dead
adopters:        Michael & Mary (or May) Moran of FR Co
new name:        Alice Delaney Moran
references:      CR 30: 88        J 40: 510
date:            16 Nov 1893
    *
adoptee:         Clyde Depoy (or Depay ?) aged 5Y on
                 25 Aug 1894 (22 Aug 1893 also used)
parents:         Anthony & Nellie Depoy, father dead
adopters:        Thomas J & Mary A Fetters of FR Co
new name:        Clyde Fetters
references:      CR 30: 90        J 40: 540
date:            25 Nov 1893
    *
adoptee:         Agness Ryan aged 3W on 23 Dec 1893
parents:         John & Sarah Ryan, mother dead
adopters:        John & Johanna Faherty (or Flaherty ?)
                 of FR Co
new name:        Agnes Faherty (or Flaherty)
references:      CR 30: 92        J 41: 29
date:            20 Dec 1893
    *
adoptee:         Edwin Every aged 14M on 6 Jan 1894
parents:         Henry & Anna Eliza Every, mother died on
                 19 Sep 1893
adopters:        Henry C & Mary B Eccles of FR Co
new name:        Edwin Johnston Eccles
references:      CR 30: 94        J 41: 49
date:            30 Dec 1893
    *
adoptee:         Dorothy Danenhower aged 8Y
parents:         father-Charles N Danenhower of Cincinnati
                 mother-Mary Isidor Danenhower, wife of
                 the above, died about 4 years prior
adopters:        Inez Okey, unmarried, of Columbus,
                 Inez was a sister of Mary Isidor Danenhower,
                 Inez had been caring for the child
new name:        Dorothy Okey
references:      CR 30: 84        J 41: 59
date:            3 Jan 1894
    *

adoptee:            Pearl Nagle (or Nagel) aged 5Y on 13 May
                    1893
parents:            George M & Josephine Nagle, both dead
adopters:           Charles L & Flora A Schneider of FR Co
new name:           Pauline Adele Schneider
references:         CR 30: 195          J 41: 185
date:               10 Feb 1894
                    a John H Nagle was appointed by the court
                    as the child's "next friend;"  a Virginia
                    Nagle served as a witness
        *
adoptee:            _____ Edwards (no first name) aged 3W
                    on 20 Mar 1894
parents:            Bell(e) Edwards
adopters:           Albert C & Zina M Young of FR Co
new name:           Clarence Adel Young
references:         CR 30: 415          J 41: 302
date:               19 Mar 1894
        *
adoptee:            Phyllis Cornelia Keck aged 6Y on 5 Dec
                    1893
parents:            Christopher & Ollivia Keck, mother dead
adopters:           John C & Lizzie DeWitt of Summit Co, OH
new name:           Phyllis Cornelia DeWitt
references:         CR 30: 413          J 41: 442
date:               21 Apr 1894
        *
adoptee:            Marion Elizabeth Boyd aged 6W on 10 May
                    1894
parents:            Absolom F & Cornelia M Boyd
adopters:           Matthias D & Ada A Bradley of FR Co
new name:           Marion Elizabeth Bradley
references:         CR 30: 454          J 41: 502
date:               9 May 1894
        *
adoptee:            Sylvia (or Silvia) Celia Sheehan aged 3Y
                    on 12 Aug 1894
parents:            Mrs Katie Smith, father dead
adopters:           John Henry (middle name) & Jennie E Moehl
                    of FR Co
new name:           Sylvia Celia Moehl
references:         CR 30: 586          J 42: 80
date:               21 Jun 1894
        *
adoptee:            Charles Henry Miller aged 8Y on __ Oct
                    1894
parents:            unknown, child was a ward of the Chicago
                    Home of the Friendless (Ill.), A. C.
                    Bartlett, Pres.
adopters:           Justin & Ida J (or T ?) Pinney of
                    Worthington, FR Co
new name:           Pheny Gorden Pinney
references:         CR 30: 584          J 42: 91

| | |
|---|---|
| date: | 26 Jun 1894 |

\*

| | |
|---|---|
| adoptee: | Charles Mutispaugh aged 1Y on 1 Aug 1894 |
| parents: | Emmil (or Emmit ?) Mogan,    Mary Mutispaugh |
| adopters: | George C & Lizzie Dell (or Dill ?) Williams of Wood Co, OH |
| new name: | George Clyde Williams |
| references: | CR 30: 588      J 42: 124 |
| date: | 7 Jul 1894 |

\*

| | |
|---|---|
| adoptee: | Carrie Ester Booth aged 8Y on 25 Dec 1894 |
| parents: | Nelson H & Kate Booth, mother dead |
| adopters: | Peter & Caroline Trott of FR Co |
| new name: | |
| references: | CR 30: 590      J 42: 118 |
| date: | 7 Jul 1894 |

\*

| | |
|---|---|
| adoptee: | Elmer Baker aged 3Y on 20 Jul 1894 |
| parents: | unknown, child was a ward of the FR Co Children's Home |
| adopters: | George & Lucy Ellen Acton of FR Co |
| new name: | George Elmer Acton |
| references: | CR 31: 121      J 42: 194 |
| date: | 27 Jul 1894 |

\*

| | |
|---|---|
| adoptee: | Edna Hornet (or Homet ?) aged 6Y on __ Nov 1894 |
| parents: | both dead (see below) |
| adopters: | J Edward & Mary K Minnick of FR Co |
| new name: | Edna Pearl Minnick |
| references: | CR 35: 286      J 42: 238 |
| date: | 11 Aug 1894 |
| | child was placed in the custody of the adopters at age 4M via an indenture through the FR Co Board of Infirmary Directors until child was 16 years of age; child was the dau of Edward Gurvin (or Gurrin, Guerin ?) & _____ Smith |

\*

| | |
|---|---|
| adoptee: | Lillie Marie Vincant aged 5Y on 28 Oct 1895 |
| parents: | _____ & Margaret Vincant (first name of father not given) |
| adopters: | Horatio & Mary Mather of FR Co |
| new name: | Lillie Marie Mather |
| references: | J 42: 482 |
| date: | 1 Nov 1894 |

\*

| | |
|---|---|
| adoptee: | _____ Morgan (no first name) aged 2½M on 12 Nov 1894 |
| parents: | Mary Jane Morgan |
| adopters: | Thomas E & Martha Shrives (or Shrieves) of FR Co |

| | |
|---|---|
| new name: | Lee Fay Shrives (or Shrieves) |
| references: | CR 31: 551        J 42: 504 |
| date: | 12 Nov 1894 |

\*

| | |
|---|---|
| adoptee: | _____ Davis (no first name) born 2 Nov 1894 |
| parents: | Carrie E Davis |
| adopters: | Mahlon A & Margaret Brintlinger of FR Co |
| new name: | Gladys Brintlinger |
| references: | CR 31: 386        J 42: 564 |
| date: | 27 Nov 1894 |

\*

| | |
|---|---|
| adoptee: | Grace Schneider aged 5Y on 18 Feb 1895 |
| parents: | Jacob & Florence Schneider of Canton, OH [Stark Co] |
| adopters: | Richard D & Nancy L Stockdale of FR Co |
| new name: | Grace Stockdale |
| references: | CR 31: 380        J 42: 592 |
| date: | 6 Dec 1894 |

\*

| | |
|---|---|
| adoptee: | Nelly (or Nellie) Taylor aged 17Y on 30 Jan 1894 |
| parents: | both dead, not named |
| adopters: | Frederick & Emlie (or Emilie) Boehrig of FR Co |
| new name: | Emma Boehrig |
| references: | CR 31: 378        J 43: 121 |
| date: | 8 Jan 1895 |

\*

| | |
|---|---|
| adoptee: | Grace A Galvin aged 4Y on 9 Dec 1894 |
| parents: | George & Barbara Galvin, both dead George approved of this adoption in his will |
| adopters: | George & Elizabeth Daeumler of FR Co |
| new name: | Grace Galvin Daeumler |
| references: | CR 31: 382        J 43: 163 |
| date: | 18 Jan 1895 |

\*

| | |
|---|---|
| adoptee: | Joseph Bennett aged 9Y on 14 Feb 1894 |
| parents: | unknown |
| adopters: | William H & Mary E Ranger of FR Co |
| new name: | Walter Ranger |
| references: | CR 31: 569        J 43: 480 |
| date: | 17 Feb 1895 |

\*

| | |
|---|---|
| adoptee: | Ruth Ferrell (or Farrell) aged 1Y on 5 May 1895 |
| parents: | Lizzie O Ferrell (or Farrell) of Chippewa Lake, OH |
| adopters: | John W & Ada B Johnson of FR Co |
| new name: | Ruth Johnson |
| references: | CR 31: 571        J 43: 285 |
| date: | 25 Feb 1895 |

\*

```
adoptee:        name unknown, aged 17M on 2 Mar 1895
parents:        unknown
adopters:       George W & May Wilson of FR Co
new name:       Harley J Wilson
references:     CR 31: 575          J 43: 316
date:           4 Mar 1895
        *
adoptee:        Nellie Florence Euke aged 11Y on 25 Jan
                1895
parents:        Ferdinand & Ada Euke
adopters:       George W & Emma B Culverwell of FR Co
new name:       Nellie Florence Culverwell
references:     CR 31: 573          J 43: 342
date:           12 Mar 1895
        *
adoptee:        Albert Orville Green
parents:
adopters:       Wesley H & Anna E Ogle
new name:
references:                         J 43: 352
date:           16 Mar 1895
        *
adoptee:        Hazel Lenora (or Lenore) _____ (no last
                name given), aged 5Y on 13 Jul 1895
parents:        unknown
adopters:       William & Mary E Boeshans of FR Co
new name:       Hazel Lenore Boeshans
references:     CR 31: 557          J 43: 357
date:           18 Mar 1895
        *
adoptee:        Eva Goldie _____ (last name unknown)
                aged 2Y on 15 Aug 1895
parents:        unknown
adopters:       Charles E & Luella Hite of FR Co
new name:       Eva Goldie Hite
references:     CR 31: 549          J 43: 360
date:           19 Mar 1895
        *
adoptee:        Florence C _____ (last name unknown)
                aged 2Y on 3 May 1895
parents:        unknown
adopters:       James & Kate (or Katie) Fleming of FR Co
new name:       Florence Catharine Fleming
references:     CR 31: 559          J 43: 360
date:           19 Mar 1895
        *
adoptee:        Hellena (or Helena) Irene Curtis aged
                2Y on 17 Jul 1895
parents:        Mr. & Mrs. Curtis
adopters:       Edward & Lillian M Selby of FR Co
new name:       Helena Lucile Selby
references:     CR 31: 567          J 43: 405
date:           30 Mar 1895
        *
```

adoptee:         Mabele (or Mabel, Mable) Beatrice Smullem
                 aged 14Y on 30 Jan 1895
parents:         F M & Mary C Smullem, mother now known as
                 Mary C Page, remarried to Leonard S Page
adopters:        Leonard S & Mary C Page of FR Co
new name:        Mabel Beatrice Page
references:      CR 31: 565        J 43: 504
date:            23 Apr 1895
     *

adoptee:         Laura (or Lura) Groves, records said that
                 her last name was unknown
parents:         unknown
adopters:        W A(or H) & Rosa G Coyle of FR Co
new name:        Laura Groves Coyle
references:      CR 31: 561        J 44: 23
date:            27 May 1895
     *

adoptee:         Lillie Ethel Lasher aged 9Y on 12 Aug
                 1894
parents:         George & Malinda Lasher
adopters:        Robert & Susie Candy of FR Co
new name:        Lillie Ethel Candy
references:      CR 31: 553        J 44: 90
date:            17 Jun 1895
     *

adoptee:         Katie Schenck aged 17Y on 1 Mar 1895 &
                 Anna Schenck aged 15Y on 23 May 1895
parents:         John & Katharina Schenck
adopters:        Heinrich (or Henry) & Katharine (or
                 Katharina) Frohenberg of FR Co
new name:        Katie & Anna Frohenberg
references:      CR 31: 555        J 44: 92
date:            18 Jun 1895
     *

adoptee:         Nyra Lucas aged 6Y on 13 Jan 1895
parents:         Darius L & Minnie E Lucas
adopters:        George & Cora A Crawford of FR Co
new name:        Nyra Lucelia (or Lucilia) Crawford
references:      CR 31: 563        J 44: 116
date:            24 Jun 1895
     *

adoptee:         Bessie King aged 3Y on 15 Oct 1894
parents:         Robert & Sallie King, mother dead
adopters:        Richard H & Lydia A Vint of FR Co
new name:        Lila Bessie Vint
references:      CR 31: 607        J 44: 123
date:            26 Jun 1895
     *

adoptee:         name unknown, aged 8Y on 15(or 13) Mar
                 1896
parents:         unknown
adopters:        Solomon J & Fannie V Woolley of FR Co
new name:        Harold Dean Woolley (Harold Dean may have

been the boy's name prior to adoption?)

references:    CR 29: 587    J 44: 249

date:    3 Aug 1895

      *

adoptee:    Eleanor Guyer aged 10Y on 16 Jul 1895

parents:    Charles & Nora Guyer

adopters:    Luke G & Rose M Byrne of FR Co

new name:    Eleanor Byrne

references:    CR 31: 605    J 44: 313

date:    22 Aug 1895

      *

adoptee:    name unknown, aged 3Y on 19 Apr 1896

parents:    unknown

adopters:    John F & Alice Daugherty of FR Co

new name:    Mable Beatrice Daugherty

references:    CR 31: 603    J 44: 405

date:    21 Sep 1895

      *

adoptee:    John Ruby aged 3Y on 25 Nov 1894

parents:    Cora Ruby, child was a ward of the FR Co Children's home

adopters:    Gardiner A & Jennie A Goble of FR Co

new name:    Chester William Goble

references:    CR 33: 605    J 44: 427

date:    30 Sep 1895

      *

adoptee:    Clara Worcester Canfield

parents:    none mentioned; a guardian was appointed over Clara by the Cuyahoga Co., OH, Probate Court prior to 12 July 1895, unknown to the adopters. The adopters were seeking a reversal of an earlier adoption [in Cuyahoga Co. ?] and name change for the best interest of Clara in legal matters in Cuyahoga Co. Name of child was changed back to Clara Worcester Canfield. Adoption negated.

adopters:    James F & Jane Worcester of FR Co

new name:    see above comments

references:    CR 29: 591    J 44: 173, 479, 487, 490

date:    14 Oct 1895

      *

adoptee:    name unknown, aged 3Y on 17 May 1896

parents:    unknown

adopters:    Henry & Barbara A Anthony of FR Co

new name:    Ester Elizabeth Anthony

references:    CR 29: 589    J 44: 501

date:    19 Oct 1895

      *

adoptee:    Katie Haines aged 3M on 31 Oct 1895

parents:    John & Jessie Haines

adopters:    Frederick Herman (middle name) & Johannah Hischke of FR Co

```
new name:        Katie Hischke
references:      CR 32: 270          J 45: 304
date:            29 Jan 1896
        *

adoptee:         Florence Anna Buck aged 5Y on 20 Jul 1896
parents:         Christopher & Emma Buck
adopters:        W S & Georgiana Simpkins of Ashtabula Co,
                 OH
new name:        Florence Anna Simpkins
references:      CR 34: 429          J 46: 268
date:            17 Jun 1896
        *

adoptee:         Nellie May [possibly a last name ?] aged
                 2Y on 2 Feb 1897
parents:         unknown
adopters:        William & Susanna Norton of FR Co
new name:        Nellie May Norton
references:      CR 34: 427          J 46: 321
date:            1 July 1896
        *

adoptee:         Dewitt Tallmadge Wolfrey aged 7W on
                 25 Aug 1896
parents:         Arthur W & Margaret F Wolfrey
adopters:        Christopher & Marie L F Neuner of FR Co
new name:        Carl Otto Neuner
references:      CR 34: 425          J 46: 532
date:            29 Aug 1896
        *

adoptee:         Charlotte Joerding aged 20Y on 2 Jan 1896
parents:         Frederick & Anna Maria (or Louisa)
                 Joerding; child had been in the custody
                 of the Joerdings since her 6th year
adopters:        Charles & Louisa Andre of FR Co
new name:        Charlotte Andre
references:      CR 35: 197          J 46: 575
date:            8 Sep 1896
        *

adoptee:         Carrie May Conklin aged 3Y on 16 Feb 1896
parents:         Edwy(?) Raymond (middle name) & Mary C
                 Conklin
adopters:        Peter A & Maggie Conklin of FR Co
new name:        no name change
references:      CR 35: 199          J 47: 297
date:            12 Nov 1896
        *

adoptee:         Martha Fay Barthman aged 7Y on 21 Mar 1896
                 Oliver P Barthman aged 5Y on 15 Jul 1896
parents:         John W & Julia A Barthman, mother dead
adopters:        Lemuel E & Hattie Williams of FR Co
new name:        Martha Fay Williams & Oliver P Williams
references:      CR 34: 605          J 47: 317
date:            18 Nov 1896
        *
```

adoptee:        Amelia Sophia Hoefer aged 9Y on 20 Jan
                1896
parents:        Henry & Carrie Hoefer, both dead
adopters:       William J & Mary K Gauer of FR Co
new name:       Amelia Sophia Gauer
references:     CR 35: 195        J 47: 406
date:           4 Dec 1896
        *

adoptee:        Blanch(e) Edna Stump aged 5Y on 15 Jan
                1898
parents:        Emmet N & Eva May Stump, mother dead
adopters:       Patrick & Mary Menger of FR Co
new name:       Frances Menger
references:     CR 40: 33         J 51: 219
date:           3 Jan 1897
        *

adoptee:        Homer Palmer aged 3Y on 13 May 1894
parents:        both dead, child was a ward of the FR Co
                Children's Home
adopters:       Elijah H & Mary Groomes (or Grooms) of
                FR Co
new name:       Edgar Palmer Groomes (or Grooms)
references:     CR 38: 12         J 48: 225
date:           13 Feb 1897
        *

adoptee:        Doris Porter aged 6M on 13 Mar 1897
parents:        Charles  Hall, Elaine M Porter
adopters:       Mrs. H F Ware of FR Co
new name:       Doris Nevada Ware
references:     CR 38: 266        J 48: 324
date:           2 Mar 1897
        *

adoptee:        Nanna Roderick aged 3Y on 21 Dec 1896
parents:        Charles Roderick, Dora Adella Barnes
                (formerly Dora Adella Roderick)
adopters:       Mrs  Nancy M Allen, widow, of FR Co
new name:       Nanna Etta Allen
references:     CR 38: 258        J 48: 347
date:           8 Mar 1897
        *

adoptee:        Emma Fern Groom aged 8Y on 16 Feb 1897
parents:        Sherman & Nettie Groom, both dead
                Hattie Bynner was serving as the child's
                next friend
adopters:       Emma E Bynner, unmarried, of FR Co
new name:       Emma Fern Bynner
references:     CR 38: 260        J 48: 361
date:           10 Mar 1897
        *

adoptee:        Rachel Lacy aged 6Y on 15 May 1896
parents:        Mr & Mrs Lacy, child was a ward of the
                FR Co Children's Home
adopters:       George W & Jennie Brooks of FR Co

new name:        Rachel Brooks
references:      CR 38: 270          J 47: 223 & 48: 482
                 Rachel was also referred to as:  Rachael
                 G Lacey in the J entry (47: 223)
date:            31 Mar 1897
     *

adoptee:         name unknown, born in March of 1897
parents:         unknown
adopters:        Charles & Dora Prettyman of FR Co
new name:        Harry Prettyman
references:      CR 38: 262          J 48: 169, 172
date:            15 May 1897
     *

adoptee:         Floyd Lefler aged 7Y on 20 Jan 1898
parents:         Ella Neiswander
adopters:        Fred W & Corda ( or Carla ?) S Graham
new name:        Floyd Lefler Graham
references:      CR 38: 272          J 49: 296
date:            9 June 1897
     *

adoptee:         Elmer Reasoner aged 13Y on 6 Aug 1896
parents:         John & Mary Reasoner
                 the child was in the FR Co Children's
                 Home
adopters:        Edward J & Florence Ury of FR Co
new name:        Elmer Ury
references:      CR 38: 268          J 50: 133
date:            16 Aug 1897
     *

adoptee:         Willie (or William) Patno aged 4Y on
                 9 Dec 1897
parents:         Frank Patno, Anna E Wolf
adopters:        Peter H & Margaret A Wolf of FR Co
new name:        Willie Wolf
references:      CR 38: 264          J 50: 151
date:            19 Aug 1897
     *

adoptee:         John Frederick Willeke   (no ages)
                 William Joseph Willeke
                 Mary Elizabeth Willeke
parents:         Frederick C & Barbara Willeke
adopters:        Charles E Willeke of FR Co
new name:        no changes
references:      CR 38: 274          J 50: 189
date:            1 Sep 1897
     *

adoptee:         Mildred Snyder aged 3Y on 10 Sep 1897
parents:         Charles H & Roby Dell Snyder
adopters:        George H & Cora A Crawford of FR Co
new name:        Roby Crawford
references:                          J 50: 220
date:            10 Sep 1897
     *

adoptee:        John Joseph Keller aged 6Y on 16 May 1897
parents:        Joseph L & Ella Keller
adopters:       William A & Mary E Will of FR Co
new name:       John Joseph Will
references:                     J 50: 367
date:           6 Oct 1897
        *

adoptee:        Otto Dague aged 7Y on 15 Sep 1897
parents:        William & Emma Dague, Emma was dead &
                William may have been also(?)
                D B Dague was the child's guardian
adopters:       George H & Ida D Myers of FR Co
new name:       Otto Myers
references:                     J 50: 390
date:           9 Oct 1897
        *

adoptee:        Harry Jones aged 1M on 12 (or 13) Nov
                1897  (12 & 13 both used)
parents:        Peter Jackson, Cora Jones
adopters:       Noah & Carrie Cooper of FR Co
new name:       Harry Cooper
references:     CR 37: 402       J 50: 560
date:           13 Nov 1897
        *

adoptee:        Alice Laman aged 1Y on 29 Oct 1897
parents:        Rachel Laman
adopters:       O D & Mary C Tipton of FR Co
new name:       Alice Marie Tipton
references:     CR 40: 31        J 51: 105
date:           10 Dec 1897
        *

adoptee:        name unknown, aged 3Y on 10 Apr 1897
parents:        unknown, child was a ward of the FR Co
                Children's Home
adopters:       Alenson & Anna (or Annie) McDowell of
                FR Co
new name:       Ethel McDowell
references:     CR 40: 87        J 51: 491
date:           17 Feb 1898
        *

adoptee:        Lillian Shera aged 1M on 20 Apr 1898
parents:        Frank D & Dora A Shera
                an Elizabeth C Shera served as a witness
adopters:       Isaac C & Ida A Edwards of FR Co
new name:       Lillian Shera Edwards
references:     CR 40: 201       J 52: 231
date:           7 Apr 1898
        *

adoptee:        Frances Oletha Demorest aged 4Y on 11 Sep
                1897
parents:        Reward & Olga Demorest, father dead
adopters:       Clark W & Minerva E Douglas of FR Co
new name:       Frances Oletha Douglas

```
references:      CR 40: 202        J 52: 298
date:            18 Apr 1898
     *
adoptee:         Clarence Smith aged 3M on 28 May 1898
parents:         Mary Smith
adopters:        Frank & Mattie McCormick of FR Co
new name:        Clarence McCormick
references:      CR 40: 204        J 52: 457
date:            12 May 1898
     *
adoptee:         Margaret Emmerling aged 8M on 23 May 1898
parents:         John C & Margaret Emmerling, mother dead
adopters:        Joseph F & Anna M Kern of FR Co
new name:        Margaret Elsie Kern
references:      CR 40: 501        J 52: 468
date:            17 May 1898
     *
adoptee:         Gertrude B Higginson aged 10Y on 2 Aug
                 1897
parents:         John & Mary A Higginson
adopters:        Jacob A & Mary A Schreiner of FR Co
new name:        Gertrude B Schreiner
references:      CR 40: 500        J 52: 540
date:            27 May 1898
     *
adoptee:         Eugene Price aged 1M on 24 June 1898
parents:         John Dellas, Lillian Price
adopters:        Sherman & Emma Brown of FR Co
new name:        Eugene Brown
references:      CR 40: 502        J 53: 38
date:            9 June 1898
     *
adoptee:         Helen Stewart aged 6Y on 21 Jul 1897
parents:         Giles & Annabel G Stewart
adopters:        Myra A Suydam (female) of FR Co
new name:        Helen Suydam
references:      CR 40: 506        J 53: 45
date:            9 Jun 1898
     *
adoptee:         Clara Esther Bowman aged 4M on 29 May
                 1898
parents:         John & Ella Bowman
adopters:        Alfred & Delia (or Della) M Potter of
                 FR Co
new name:        Clara Esther Potter
references:      CR 40: 503        J 53: 54
date:            10 June 1898
     *
adoptee:         Ruth Ella Bowman aged 4M on 29 May 1898
parents:         John & Ella Bowman
adopters:        Dexter P & Emma L Crowner of FR Co
new name:        Ruth Ella Crowner
references:      CR 40: 505        J 53: 53
```

```
date:              10 Jun 1898
   *
adoptee:           name unknown, aged 2Y on 25 Dec 1897
                   (1898 also used)
parents:           unknown
adopters:          George H & Mamie M Gill of Columbus
new name:          Hazel Margaret Gill
references:        CR 40: 507        J 53: 242
date:              19 Jul 1898
                   child was a ward of the Children Home
                   Society of Ohio, Dr. F H Darby, Supt
   *
adoptee:           Ida M Pinney aged 14Y on 1 Sep 1898
parents:           Nathan & Henrietta Pinney, mother dead
adopters:          Justin & Ida M Pinney of FR Co
new name:          no name change
references:        CR 43: 6          J 53: 423
date:              17 Aug 1898
   *
adoptee:           Nellie Thompson aged 5Y on 2 Sep 1898
parents:           William Thompson
adopters:          John B & Rose Anna Christie of FR Co
new name:          Nellie Christie
references:        CR 40: 562        J 53: 545
date:              8 Sep 1898
   *
adoptee:           name unknown, aged 6M on 23 Aug 1898
parents:           unknown
adopters:          Thomas & Sarah Jane Hart of FR Co
new name:          Raymond Bertrand Hart
references:        CR 40: 560        J 54: 30, 33
date:              12 Sep 1898
   *
adoptee:           Joseph Leo Hennis aged 3Y on 4 Feb 1898
parents:           Edward L & Clara B Hennis, mother dead
adopters:          Magdalena Sagstetter of FR Co
new name:          Joseph Leo Sagstetter
references:        CR 40: 561        J 54: 68
date:              22 Sep 1898
                   John T Sagsetter (probably should read
                   Sagstetter) served as next friend
   *
adoptee:           Helen Taylor aged 5M on 8 Sep 1898
parents:           Charles Andrews, Ella Taylor
adopters:          Michael & Effie Leger of FR Co
new name:          Helen E Leger
references:        CR 40: 498        J 54: 94
date:              26 Sep 1898
   *
adoptee:           Anna C Rush aged 8M on 28 Sep 1898
parents:           John L & Mary C Rush
adopters:          John V & Mary A Orb of FR Co
new name:          Anna C Orb
```

references: CR 40: 497     J 54: 117
date:       30 Sep 1898
     *

adoptee:    George Martin Locke aged 4M on ___ Oct
            1898 (no day given)
parents:    Martin G & Mary A Locke, father dead
adopters:   George & Edith N Kehm, Jr. of FR Co
new name:   Francis William Kehm
references: CR 40: 604     J 54: 244
date:       20 Oct 1898
     *

adoptee:    Mary Jones aged 6Y on 8 Oct 1898
parents:    unknown
adopters:   Torrence J & Emeroy Parish of FR Co
new name:   Ethel Parish
references: CR 43: 7     J 54: 486
date:       28 Nov 1898
            child was a ward of the FR Co Children's
            Home

     *

adoptee:    name unknown, child was called "May
            Fourth" because she was found on the
            4th of May 1895, aged 3Y on 4 May 1899
parents:    unknown, child was a ward of the FR Co
            Children's Home
adopters:   George C & Irene Fidler of FR Co
new name:   Nellie May Belle Fidler
references: CR 43: 4     J 55: 21
date:       17 Dec 1898
     *

adoptee:    Homer Ellsworth Newton aged 9Y on 20
            Jan 1899
parents:    Denny H & Mary Newton
adopters:   G W & Harriet A Bigelow of FR Co
new name:   Homer Ellsworth Bigelow
references: CR 40: 605     J 55: 112
date:       31 Dec 1898
     *

adoptee:    Mary Elizabeth Newton aged 12Y on 6 Jan
            1899
parents:    Denny H & Mary Newton
adopters:   G W & Harriet A Bigelow of FR Co
new name:   Mary Elizabeth Bigelow
references: CR 40: 606     J 55: 114
date:       31 Dec 1898
     *

adoptee:    Earl Krim aged 11Y on 4 Aug 1898
parents:    William C (or E) Krim, Mrs. Eva McMillen
adopters:   Mrs. Jennie Krim of FR Co
new name:   Earl Dean Krim
references: CR 43: 5     J 55: 125
date:       3 Jan 1899
     *

adoptee:        Lorhetta May Ashenfelter aged 1Y on 26
                Jan 1899
parents:        Joseph Walter (middle name) & Arkansas
                Lee Ashenfelter (husband & wife)
adopters:       Dennis E & Lulu May Hedrick of FR Co
new name:       Lorhetta May Hedrick
references:     CR 43: 10        J 55: 403
date:           15 Feb 1899
       *
adoptee:        Florence C Kelly aged 11Y on 27 Sep 1899
                William E Kelly aged 5Y on 6 Feb 1899
parents:        Lawrence & Susan A Kelly, mother dead
adopters:       W G  & Ida V Spitler of FR Co
new name:       Florence C & William E Spitler
references:     CR 43: 13        J 55: 530
date:           1 Mar 1899
       *
adoptee:        Virginia Elizabeth Clark aged 4W
parents:        Linnie Clark (mother)
adopters:       F M (or W) & Jennie E Jackson of FR Co
new name:       Virginia Elizabeth Jackson
references:     CR 43: 8         J 55: 586
date:           6 Mar 1899
                a Frank D Jackson served as a witness
       *
adoptee:        name unknown, aged 2M on 23 Feb 1899
parents:        unknown
adopters:       William & Carrie Kleinlein of FR Co
new name:       Wilbur David Kleinlein
references:     CR 43: 14        J 55: 585
date:           6 Mar 1899
       *
adoptee:        Russell Benedict aged 16M on 2 Apr 1899
parents:        John W & Minnie Benedict
adopters:       Joshua & Sarah Swickard of FR Co
new name:       Russell Swickard
references:     CR 43: 9          J 56: 227
date:           10 Apr 1899
       *
adoptee:        Doris Benedict aged 3Y on 20 Oct 1898
parents:        John W & Minnie Benedict
adopters:       Joshua & Sarah Swickard of FR Co
new name:       Doris Swickard
references:     CR 43: 11        J 56: 227
date:           10 Apr 1899
       *
adoptee:        Ada Belle Ormes (or Armes) aged 6M on
                13 May 1899
parents:        Virgie Ormes
adopters:       John & Amanda Stagg(s) of FR Co
new name:       Ada Belle Staggs
references:     CR 43: 15        J 56: 293
date:           26 Apr 1899
       *

| | |
|---|---|
| adoptee: | Harry Thomas aged 4Y on 6 Mar 1899 |
| parents: | William & Maud Thomas, mother dead |
| adopters: | Leo G & Mary M Brockhoven (or Brock-haven) of FR Co |
| new name: | Harry Thomas Brockhoven (or Brockhaven) |
| references: | CR 43: 37      J 56: 321 |
| date: | 29 Apr 1899 |

*

| | |
|---|---|
| adoptee: | Hazel Virginia Crethers aged 5Y on 25 Dec 1898 |
| parents: | John H & Elizabeth Virginia Crethers |
| adopters: | Amanda Bronson of FR Co |
| new name: | Hazel Virginia Bronson |
| references: | J 56: 383 |
| date: | 9 May 1899 |

*

| | |
|---|---|
| adoptee: | John K Crethers aged 4Y on 18 Feb 1899 |
| parents: | John H & Elizabeth Virginia Crethers |
| adopters: | Amanda Bronson of FR Co |
| new name: | John K Bronson |
| references: | J 56: 384 |
| date: | 9 May 1899 |

*

| | |
|---|---|
| adoptee: | Marie Stanslus (or Stanlus) Dunlap aged 8Y on 8 Sep 1898 |
| parents: | James & Jennie Dunlap, father dead |
| adopters: | Michael J & Mary A Rafferty of FR Co |
| new name: | Marie Stanslus Rafferty |
| references: | CR 43: 42      J 56: 395 |
| date: | 11 May 1899 |

*

| | |
|---|---|
| adoptee: | Ethel Lina Bentz aged 2Y on 26 Mar 1899 |
| parents: | unknown |
| adopters: | William H & Julia Wolfel of FR Co |
| new name: | Ethel Lina Wolfel |
| references: | J 56: 449 |
| date: | 19 May 1899 |

*

| | |
|---|---|
| adoptee: | Roy Haddock aged 3Y on 10 Apr 1899 |
| parents: | Clara Haddock |
| adopters: | Seymore & Emma Polley of FR Co |
| new name: | Roy Polley |
| references: | J 56: 527 |
| date: | 3 Jun 1899 |

*

| | |
|---|---|
| adoptee: | name unknown, aged ca 14M, a native of FR Co |
| parents: | unknown |
| adopters: | Darius J & Mattie L Burnham of Madison Co, OH |
| new name: | Martha Evaline Burnham |
| references: | CR 43: 32      J 57: 113 |
| date: | 6 Jul 1899 |

*

adoptee:          George Lang aged 16Y on 30 Mar 1899
parents:          John Crow, Julia Lang
adopters:         George & Julia Lang (same Julia as above)
                  of FR Co
new name:
references:       CR 43: 34        J 57: 185
date:             18 Jul 1899
      *

adoptee:          Julia Crow aged 6Y on 23 May 1899
parents:          George & Abalonia Crow
adopters:         George & Julia Lang of FR Co
new name:         Julia Lang
references:       CR 43: 38        J 57: 185
date:             18 Jul 1899
      *

adoptee:          Lucille Gertrude Garner aged 1M on 18 Aug
                  1899
parents:          Myrtle Belle Garner
adopters:         William F & Nellie Volk of FR Co
new name:         Lucille Gertrude Volk
references:       CR 43: 35        J 57: 321
date:             18 Aug 1899
      *

adoptee:          Katharine Agnes Clark aged 8Y on 22 Aug
                  1899
parents:          Joel & Katharine Clark
adopters:         Richard M & Mary A Peckham of FR Co
new name:         Katharine Agnes Clark Peckham
references:       CR 43: 31        J 57: 405
date:             6 Sep 1899
      *

adoptee:          Minnie May Roby aged 10Y on 13 Jun 1899
parents:          Cora McDonnel, formerly Cora Ruby;
                  Cora married John McDonnel on 7 Jul 1893
adopters:         John D & Cora McDonnel of FR Co
new name:         Minnie May McDonnel
references:       CR 43: 36        J 57: 439
date:             14 Sep 1899
      *

adoptee:          Grace Ethel Kerwood (probably a new name)
parents:
adopters:         Mary Kerwood
new name:
references:                       J 57: 478, 491, 493
date:             25 Sep 1899, 29 Sep 1899
                  "matter to set aside"
                  adoption proceedings took place in
                  Fairfield Co, OH
                  child was placed in FR Co Children's Home
                  after being removed from Mary Kerwood
      *

adoptee:          Odra May Paine aged 5Y on 27 May 1900
parents:          William M & Olive Paine

adopters:       William H & Fannie A Crawford of FR Co
new name:       Odra May Crawford
references:     CR 47: 23         J 58: 258
date:           6 Dec 1899
        *

adoptee:        _____ Swalley aged 3W on 24 Dec 1899
parents:        Florence Swalley
adopters:       Anthony & Emma Joerger of FR Co
new name:       Chester A Joerger
references:     CR 47: 8          J 58: 335
date:           23 Dec 1899
        *

adoptee:        Mary Hill aged 6Y on 25 May 1900
parents:        Mr  & Mrs Hill, mother dead
                child was a ward of the Delaware Co, OH
                Children's Home
adopters:       Franklin H & Nancy J Wagner of FR Co
new name:       Mary N Wagner
references:     CR 47: 21         J 58: 368
date:           30 Dec 1899
        *

adoptee:        Sanford Brownlee Oare aged 5Y on 4 Jul 1899
                (1900 also used)
parents:        William & Malinda Oare
adopters:       John & Ida Sokoff of FR Co
new name:       Sanford Brownlee Sokoff
references:     CR 47: 13         J 58: 549
date:           1 Feb 1900
        *

adoptee:        Myrtle Fortner aged 4W on 4 Feb 1900
                born 7 Jan 1900 at Cincinnati
parents:        unknown, child was a ward of the Children's
                Home of Cincinnati, OH
adopters:       John W & Ada R Strimple of Columbus
new name:       Thelma Ellis Strimple
references:     CR 47: 12         J 58: 571
date:           5 Feb 1900
        *

adoptee:        Leona Andrews aged 5Y on 6 Nov 1899
parents:        Orvill(e) & Lola Andrews
adopters:       William H & Anna Young of FR Co
new name:       Leona May Young
references:     CR 47: 5          J 59: 35
date:           12 Feb 1900
        *

adoptee:        Mary Githens aged 15Y on 21 May 1899
parents:        Joseph & Anna Githens
adopters:       J A & Ellen Weinland of FR Co
new name:       Mary Weinland
references:     CR 47: 24         J 59: 246
date:           19 Mar 1900
        *

adoptee:      Winnie Marie Oare aged 9M on 21 Mar 1900
parents:      William & Malinda Oare
adopters:     George W & Ida B Fields of FR Co
new name:     Winifred Ruth Fields
references:   CR 47: 17        J 59: 250
date:         20 Mar 1900
    *
adoptee:      Edith May Swelly (or Selley ?) aged 2Y
              on 28 mar 1900
parents:      Florence Swelly (or Selly ?)
              comment: child's surname appeared to be
              "May" in the records, but was probably
              Swelly or Selly; it was indexed as Edith
              May
adopters:     William C & Julia Ann Jones of FR Co
new name:     Willie Julia Jones
references:   CR 50: 247       J 59: 440
date:         17 Apr 1900
    *
adoptee:      Ada Helen Howe aged 2Y
parents:      Ada Howe
adopters:     William H & Kate R (or B) Harding of FR Co
new name:     Violet Marie Harding
references:   CR 47: 11        J 59: 555
date:         3 May 1900
    *
adoptee:      Armsford Evans aged 12Y on 6 May 1900
parents:      George Yocum, Laura Evans
adopters:     Thomas & Bessie Finnegan of Guernsey Co, OH
new name:     Armsford Evans Finnegan
references:   CR 47: 16        J 60: 10
date:         8 May 1900
    *
adoptee:      Oscar Earl Tevlin aged 5Y on 7 Oct 1900
parents:      Patrick & Lottie Tevlin, mother dead
adopters:     Alexander & Louisa McKenna of FR Co
new name:     Oscar Earl McKenna
references:   CR 47: 14        J 60: 30, 31
date:         11 May 1900
    *
adoptee:      Charles Harrison Switzer aged 11Y on 6 Apr
              1899 (1900 also used)
parents:      Frank & Minnie Hughes Switzer
adopters:     William E & Susanna Evans of FR Co
new name:     Charles Harrison Evans
references:   CR 47: 6         J 60: 45
date:         14 May 1900
              comment: mother also referred to as just
              Minnie Hughes
    *
adoptee:      unknown, aged 4Y on 23 Dec 1897 (1899 also
              used)
parents:      unknown, see next page

according to entries in the J, N W Weidel was the father; child was a ward of the FR Co Children's Home or was put there

adopters: Nicholas Weidle of FR Co
"no wife living"
new name: Frederick Virgil Weidle
references: CR 47: 4          J 61: 353
date: 28 May 1900
    *

adoptee: Florence Bush aged 7M on 25 Jun 1900
parents: _____ Bush & Mrs. Jessie Bush (first name of Mr. Bush unknown)
adopters: John F & Mary Paynter of FR Co
new name: Florence Ruth Paynter
references: CR 47: 9          J 60: 326
date: 29 Jun 1900
    *

adoptee: Lulu May Jefferson Phipps aged 10Y on ___ May 1900; adopted child of Ella Phipps
parents: none given other than adopted mother above
adopters: C J & Martha Wright of FR Co
new name: Lulu Phipps Wright
references: J 60: 438, 484, 529, 530
date: 21 Jul 1900
Elizabeth R Bass detained the child, writ of habeas corpus filed by the Wrights, Ella Phipps said to be the mother of Lulu, adoption vacated, petition against Elizabeth R Bass dismissed, child apparently returned to Ella Phipps
    *

adoptee: Frederick Lee Gouldner aged 8Y on 17 Nov 1899
parents: Michael & Olive Gouldner
adopters: James & Sarah L Swank of FR Co
new name: name to remain the same
references: CR 47: 18          J 60: 508
date: 4 Aug 1900
    *

adoptee: James Francis Gouldner aged 10 Y on 31 Apr 1900
parents: Michael & Olive Gouldner
adopters: James & Sarah Swank of FR Co
new name: name to remain the same
references: CR 47: 19          J 60: 509
date: 4 Aug 1900
    *

adoptee: Arthur Cassube aged 12Y on 11 Aug 1900
parents: Joseph & Julia Cassube, mother dead
adopters: William Cassube of FR Co
new name:
references: CR 47: 7          J 61: 59
date: 1 Sep 1900
    *

adoptee:        Ralph Gillett aged 2Y on 14 Oct 1900
parents:        Arthur & Mary Gillett
adopters:       Charles N & Katie Lynn of FR Co
new name:       Ralph Lynn
references:     CR 47: 2          J 61: 102
date:           12 Sep 1900
        *

adoptee:        Maud May Moss aged 12Y on 22 Aug 1900
parents:        Theodore T & Mary F Moss, divorced about
                8Y prior
adopters:       Edward & Frances Getreu of FR Co
new name:       Maud May Getreu
references:     CR 47: 1          J 61: 176
date:           25 Sep 1900
        *

adoptee:        Charlotte Lucille Beecher aged 9Y on 20
                May 1900
parents:        Amos W & Carrie Freeman Beecher
adopters:       Henry F & Mary C Crawford of FR Co
new name:       Charlotte B Crawford
references:     CR 47: 3          J 61: 345
date:           27 Oct 1900
        *

adoptee:        Beatrice May Cook aged 10M on 8 Nov 1900
parents:        John & Georgia (or Georgie) Cook
adopters:       Joseph & Lydia Conn of FR Co
new name:       Beatrice May Conn
references:                       J 61: 469
date:           20 Nov 1900
        *

adoptee:        Joseph Hayes aged 1Y on 24 Dec 1900
parents:        Adeline Hayes
adopters:       Thomas P & Elizabeth Hays of FR Co
new name:       no mention of a name change
references:                       J 62: 155
date:           4 Jan 1901
        *

adoptee:        John Reens aged 10Y on 28 Aug 1900
parents:        Jasper & Bertha Reens, mother dead
adopters:       Graham & Lottie Shaw of FR Co
new name:       John H Shaw
references:                       J 62: 221, 222
date:           14 Jan 1901
        *

adoptee:        Helen Koenig aged 3Y on 4 Jan 1900
parents:        Katie Koenig
adopters:       William & Catharine Brown of FR Co
new name:       Helen Sarah Brown
references:                       J 62: 232
date:           15 Jan 1901
        *

adoptee:        Frances Elizabeth Stiltz aged 1Y on 26
                May 1901

parents:          adopted child of Oleveya M Stiltz
adopters:         C F & Catharine E Lew of FR Co
new name:         Frances Elizabeth Lew
references:                  J 62: 255
date:             19 Jan 1901
     *

adoptee:          _____ Wadkins aged 4M on 10 Jan 1901
parents:          Angie Wadkins
adopters:         Reuben & Mary Kelley of FR Co
new name:         Mendee (or Wendee ?) Kelley
references:                  J 62: 286
date:             24 Jan 1901
     *

adoptee:          Daisy E Sines aged 4M on 23 Jan 1901
parents:          Maggie Sines
adopters:         Franklin & Ada (or Adah) Bowsher of FR Co
new name:         Daisy Eveline Bowsher
references:                  J 62: 295
date:             26 Jan 1901
     *

adoptee:          Ruby Rosella Hinds aged 5Y on 30 Oct 1901
parents:          John & _____ Hinds, mother dead
adopters:         Harry & Addie Branch of FR Co
new name:         Ruby Rosella Branch
references:                  J 62: 576
date:             18 Mar 1901
     *

adoptee:          Amos Driscoll aged 3Y on 3 Oct 1901
parents:          none mentioned
adopters:         J A & Catharine Spindler of FR Co
new name:         John Albert Spindler
references:                  J 63: 34, 37
date:             26 Mar 1901
                  child was a ward of the Children's Home
                  of Delaware Co, OH
     *

adoptee:          Mabel L Huber aged 1Y on 19 Jan 1901
parents:          Charles & Minnie Huber
adopters:         Theodore & Eleanor Crabtree of FR Co
new name:         Mabel L Crabtree
references:                  J 63: 134
date:             12 Apr 1901
     *

adoptee:          Ada Campbell aged 6Y on 22 Oct 1900
parents:          Nathen Ranger, Anna Hansbery
adopters:         Harry & Ella Ward of FR Co
new name:         Lillian Ward
references:                  J 63: 135
date:             12 Apr 1901
                  child was a ward of the FR Co Children's
                  Home
     *

adoptee:        Roy H Kinsey aged 18Y on 8 Aug 1900
parents:        none mentioned, father dead
adopters:       Alverton & Emma E Crumley
new name:       Roy H Crumley
references:                          J 63: 167, 168
date:           17 Apr 1901
          *

adoptee:        name unknown, aged 4W on 11 June 1901
parents:        unknown
adopters:       George B & Carrie C Kelly of FR Co
new name:       Anna Bell Kelly
references:     CR 47: 606      J 63: 469
date:           10 Jun 1901
          *

adoptee:        Frank Johnson aged 7Y on __ May 1902
parents:        Bessie Lewis (dead)
adopters:       Rhoda Wilson of FR Co, Rhoda was the
                grandmother of Frank Johnson
new name:       Frank Wilson
references:     CR 41: 586      J 63: 485
date:           13 Jun 1901
          *

adoptee:        Frank Bott aged 16Y on 8 Sep 1900
                (aged 17Y also used)
parents:        Frank & Anna Bott
adopters:       Henry & Anna Reiter of FR Co,
                Anna Reiter was formerly Anna Bott
new name:       Frank Reiter
references:     CR 41: 587      J 63: 584
date:           2 Jul 1901
          *

adoptee:        Bertie Leota Wood aged 1Y on 29 Sep 1901
parents:        Cullen & Sarah Wood
adopters:       George W & Ida Fields of FR Co
new name:       Blanche Fern Fields
references:     CR 41: 589      J 64: 3
date:           3 Jul 1901
          *

adoptee:        Charles R Eswine aged 5Y on 9 Nov 1900
parents:        Chas Yenmans (or Yemmans ?), Mattie
                Hershiser
adopters:       Martha J Eswine of Licking Co, OH
new name:
references:     CR 39: 602      J 64: 164
date:           2 Aug 1901
                comment:  "Charels R Eswine" may be the
                new name of the adoptee
          *

adoptee:        Ruth Ritter aged 1Y on 30 May 1901
parents:        C F Gosnell (or Gasnell ?), Lulu (or
                Lula) Ritter
adopters:       Joseph G & Almeda C Overbeck of FR Co
new name:       Doris Lydia Elizabeth Overbeck

references:      CR 47: 607        J 64: 170
date:            5 Aug 1901
        *
adoptee:         Chester Lanning aged 5M on 5 Sep 1900
                 (1901 also used)
parents:         Lena Lanning
adopters:        Isaiah & Ida Edmonds of FR Co
new name:        Chester Isaiah Edmonds
references:      CR 41: 595        J 64: 336
date:            12 Sep 1901
        *
adoptee:         Ruth L Dyton aged 3Y on 16 Apr 1901
parents:         Nettie Dyton
adopters:        D H & Debbie R Burnham of FR Co
new name:        Ruth L Burnham
references:      CR 41: 596        J 64: 368
date:            20 Sep 1901
        *
adoptee:         Bishop Ewing aged 9Y on 18 Apr 1891
                 (1901 also used)
parents:         George & Margaret Ewing
                 child was a ward of the FR Co Children's
                 Home
adopters:        Joseph & Martha Surrell (or Surell) of
                 FR Co
new name:        Bishop Ellsworth Surrell
references:      CR 41: 597        J 64: 455
date:            7 Oct 1901
        *
adoptee:         Arthur Lamb aged 4Y on 29 Mar 1901
parents:         Arthur C & Annie Lamb
                 child was a ward of the FR Co Children's
                 Home
adopters:        Samuel A & Amanda Davis of FR Co
new name:        James Walter Tod Davis
references:      CR 41: 592        J 65: 49
date:            9 Nov 1901
        *
adoptee:         Hazel Baughman aged 1Y on 30 Apr 1901
parents:         Jesse & Sarah Baughman
                 child was a ward of the FR Co Children's
                 Home
adopters:        Samuel A & Amanda Davis of FR Co
new name:        Pauline Isabelle Davis
references:      CR 41: 594        J 65: 50
date:            9 Nov 1901
        *
adoptee:         William Lynn Johnson aged 6Y on 22 Oct 1901
parents:         Harry Lynn (middle name) & Katharine
                 Johnson
adopters:        Alfretta M Fleming of FR Co
new name:        no name change mentioned
references:      CR 41: 590        J 65: 289

```
date:            24 Dec 1901
     *

adoptee:         Clyde R Wood aged 4Y on 4 Oct 1901
parents:         C R Wood
adopters:        Charles K & Davannis Anderson of FR Co
new name:        Clyde R Anderson
references:      CR 41: 591      J 65: 305
date:            24 Dec 1901
     *
```

# INDEX

ABB LICHON, Christopher 5 Lizzie 5 Mary Grace 5
ACHUFF, Lois 17 William 17
ACTON, George 31 George Elmer 31 Lucy Ellen 31
ADAMS, Bessie Gertrude 8 Esther L 8 George M 8 Jennie 7
ADKINS, Geneva 22 John 22 Nannie 22
ALLEN, Bzotas Bright 5 Catharine 13 Charles 13 Forrest 18 George W 5 Nancy M 37 Nanna Etta 37 Sarah M 18
ALLEY, Frances 3
ALTMAN, David 13 Hannah L 13 Myrtle 13
AMMONDS, Anne 9
ANDERSON, Charles K 53 Clyde R 53 Davannis 53
ANDRE, Charles 36 Charlotte 36 Louisa 36
ANDREWS, Charles 41 Leona 46 Lola 46 Orvill(e) 46
ANTHONY, Barbara A 35 Ester Elizabeth 35 Henry 35
ARMES, Ada Belle 43
ARMOR, Daisy 8
ARNETT, Effie Levisa 9 Ephraim 9 Martha Jane 9
ARNOLD, Blanch Alma 20 Charles 20 Saddie A 20
ASHBAUGH, Eliza Jane 14 Eliza Ruth 14 James R 14
ASHENFELTER, Arkansas Lee 43 Joseph Walter 43 Lorhetta May 43
BADER, Caroline 7 Emma 7 George Peter 7
BAILEY, Lizzie J 19 Martin L 19 Veloy Pearl 19
BAILY, Ann 16 George W 16 William 16
BAKER, Elmer 31
BARD, Grace 28 Martha Jane 28 William P 28
BARNES, Dora Adella 37

BARRETT, Alta May 11 Margaretta 11 William 11
BARTHMAN, John W 36 Julia A 36 Martha Fay 36 Oliver P 36
BARTLETT, A C 30
BASS, Elizabeth R 48
BATES, John 9 Lizzie 9 Peter 9
BAUGHMAN, Bertha May 18 Hattie 18 Hazel 52 Jesse 52 Kansas 18 Sarah 52
BEATHARD, J W 25 John Rosal 25 Mrs 25
BEAVERS, Alice 28 Grace 28 Nelson 28
BEEBE, Alfred 17
BEECHER, Amos W 49 Carrie Freeman 49 Charlotte Lucille 49
BELL, Cyrus C 13 Myrtie 13 Nancy 13
BENADUM, Jennie F 10
BENEDICT, Doris 43 John W 43 Minnie 43 Russell 43
BENNETT, Joseph 32
BENNS, Charles I 17 Ervin 17 Mary Ann 17
BENTZ, Ethel Lina 44
BERG, George W 16 Martha 16
BETHEL, Albert 2 John 2
BETHGE, Paul 17
BICKEL, Charles 3 John G 3 Sabina 3
BIGELOW, G W 42 Harriet A 42 Homer Ellsworth 42 Mary Elizabeth 42
BILLINGS, Estella Minnie 6 Henry M 6 Lydia A 6
BLAIN, Addison 26 Walter 26
BLAIR, Addison 26 Walter 26
BLAZER, Mrs I 23
BOEHRIG, Emilie 32 Emlie 32 Emma 32 Frederick 32
BOESHANS, Hazel Lenore 33 Mary E 33 William 33
BOLEN, Lillie 25 Urie 25
BONNETT, Andrew O 13 Myrtie 13 Rosetta M 13 Rozeta M 13
BOOTH Carrie E 31 Kate 31 Nelson H 31

55

BOTT, Anna 51 Frank 51
BOWMAN, Clara Esther 40 Ella 40 John
    40 Ruth Ella 40
BOWSHER, Ada 50 Adah 50 Daisy
    Eveline 50 Franklin 50
BOYD, Absolom F 30 Cornelia M 30
    Marion Elizabeth 30
BRADLEY, Ada A 30 Marion Elizabeth 30
    Matthias D 30
BRANCH, Addie 50 Harry 50 Ruby Rosella
    50
BRINTLINGER, Gladys 32 Mahlon A 32
    Margaret 32
BRITTINGHAM, James N 4 Minnie 4
    Sarah K 4
BROCKHAVEN, Harry Thomas 44 Leo G
    44 Mary M 44
BROCKHOVEN, Harry Thomas 44 Leo G
    44 Mary M 44
BRODBECK, Emma 15 George Frederick
    15 Olive Gertrude 15
BRONSON, Amanda 44 Hazel Virginia 44
    John K 44
BROOKS, Blanch 20 George W 37 Jennie
    37 Joseph W 20 Rachel 38 Sadie A 20
BROWN, Catharine 49 Elisha 19 Emma
    19 40 Eugene 40 Harry Clayton 19
    Helen Sarah 49 John 26 Sherman 40
    Walter 26 William 49
BROWNING, Lucinda 5 Mary Grace 5
BRYANT, Bzotas 5 Sarah M 5
BUCHHOLZ, Anna 11 Ella 11 Francis 11
    Francisca 11 Franziska 11 John 11
    Lizzie 11 Vincenz 11
BUCHOLZ, Francis 11 Francisca 11
    Franziska 11 Vincenz 11
BUCK, Christopher 36 Emma 36 Florence
    Anna 36
BUERSTLEIN, Catharine 5 Elizabeth 5
    George 5
BUERSTLINE, Georgina Catharine 5
BUMONT, Dora N 4 James D 4 Minnie 4
BURCK, Catherine 3 George 3 Margaret
    Josephine 3
BURKLEY, Augustus A 19 Elizabeth A 19
BURNETT, Frederick 10
BURNHAM, D H 52 Darius J 44 Debbie R
    52 Martha Evaline 44 Mattie L 44 Ruth
    L 52
BURTON, Emma F 16 Harriet S 16
BUSCH, George 21 Matilda 21
BUSH, Florence 48 Jessie 48
BUTT, Fannie Mary 28 Margaret 28
    Samuel 28

BYNNER, Emma E 37 Emma Fern 37
    Hattie 37
BYRD, Ananias Newton 4 John R 4 Mary
    E 4
BYRNE, Eleanor 35 Luke G 35 Rose M 35
CADWALLADER, Mabel 22 Sarah 22
CALDWELL, Ida 24 John 24 Mable 24
    Mary 24
CAMPBELL, Ada 50 Joseph 3 Mary B 3 4
    Nannie Rockey 4 P 3
CANDY, Lillie Ethel 34 Robert 34 Susie
    34
CANFIELD, Clara Worcester 35
CARPENTER, Mable 27 Mary E 27
CASE, Catharine 12 Willie 12
CASSUBE, Arthur 48 Joseph 48 Julia 48
    William 48
CHAPMAN, Edward 4 Susan 4
CHRISTIE, John B 41 Nellie 41 Rose
    Anna 41
CLARE, Annie 12 Charles 12 Clara Anne
    12 Clarence 12
CLARK, Joel 45 Julia Elizabeth 19
    Katharine Agnes 45 Linnie 43 Virginia
    Elizabeth 43
CLAYTON, Harry 19
COCKERAL, Jasper 26 Rachall 26
COCKERALL, Jasper 26 Rachall 26
    Rachel 26
COCKRELL, Blanche 26 Jasper 26 Rachal
    26 Rachall 26 Rachell 26
CODY, Bridget Elizabeth 17 Elizabeth 17
    Michael 17
COLBACH, George 26
COLLINS, Frank 14 Isabella 14 Stella
    Belle 14
CONKLIN, Carrie May 36 Edwy Raymond
    36 Maggie 36 Mary C 36 Peter A 36
CONN, Beatrice May 49 Joseph 49 Lydia
    49
CONSTANS, George F 14 Gracie Katie 14
    Katharina 14
CONWAY, Lou 14 Vevie 14
COOK, 8 14 Beatrice May 49 Fanny 8
    Georgia 49 Georgie 49 John 49
COONTS, Mable 27 Martha A 27 William
    H 27
COONTZ, Martha A 27 William H 27
COOPER, Carrie 39 Harry 39 Noah 39
CORD, Grace 25
COWGILL, Eleanor H 9 13 John 9 13
    Mary 9 William Harvey 13
COYLE, Laura Groves 34 Rosa G 34 W A
    34 W H 34

CRABTREE, Eleanor 50 Mabel L 50
Theodore 50
CRAIN, A K 15 Cora 15 Rodney 15
CRANE, Abraham K 16
CRAWFORD, Charlotte B 49 Cora A 34 38
Fannie A 46 George 34 George H 38
Henry F 49 Mary C 49 Nyra Lucelia 34
Nyra Lucilia 34 Odra May 46 Roby 38
William H 46
CRETHERS, Elizabeth Virginia 44 Hazel
Virginia 44 John H 44 John K 44
CROW, Abalonia 45 John 45 Julia 45
CROWNER, Dexter P 40 Emma L 40 Ruth
Ella 40
CROY, Almira M 7 Estella G 7 Nathan 7
CRUMLEY, Alverton 51 Emma E 51 Roy
H 51
CULVERWELL, Emma B 33 George W
33 Nellie Florence 33
CURLEY, Kate 20 Katie 20 Saddie 20
CURTIS, Helena Irene 33 Hellena Irene 33
Mr 33 Mrs 33
DAEUMLER, Elizabeth 32 George 32
Grace 32
DAGUE, D B 39 Emma 39 Otto 39 Wil-
liam 39
DALLAS, Ella R 3 Ephraim 3 Ida
Blanch(e) 3
DANENHOWER, Charles N 29 Dorothy 29
Mary Isidor 29
DARBY, F H 41
DARLING, Carrie 6 Catharine M 6 Peter 6
DAUGHERTY, Alice 35 John F 35 Mable
Beatrice 35
DAVIS, Amanda 52 Carrie 32 James Wal-
ter Tod 52 Lewis 3 Pauline Isabelle 52
Rosa Ann 3 Samuel A 52
DE WITT, John C 30 Lizzie 30 Phyllis
Cornelia 30
DELANEY, Alice 29 Ed 29 Mary 29
DELLAS, John 40
DEMOREST, Frances Oletha 39 Olga 39
Reward 39
DEPAY, Clyde 29
DEPOY, Anthony 29 Clyde 29 Nellie 29
DEVAN, Ada Florence 27 Anna 27 Annie
27 Victoria Bell 27 William 27
DEWALD, Jennie 4 John 4
DICKERSON, Anna Mary 16 Jessie 16
William W 16
DONAHUE, Julia 21 Mary Florence 21
Patrick 21
DOUGLAS, Clark W 39 Frances Oletha 39
Minerva E 39

DOYLE, Elizabeth 17 John E 17 Mary 17
DRISCOLL, Amos 50
DUNHAM, Clara Belle 19 William P 19
DUNLAP, James 44 Jennie 44 Marie Stan-
lus 44 Marie Stanslus 44
DYTON, Nettie 52 Ruth L 52
EASON, Emeline 2
EATON, Ananias Newton 4 Ann M 4 Sandy
4
ECCLES, Edwin Johnston 29 Henry C 29
Mary B 29
EDMONDS, Chester Isaiah 52 Ida 52
Isaiah 52
EDWARDS, Bell(e) 30 Ida A 39 Isaac C
39 Lillian Shera 39
EISEL, Alice F 24 William 24
EISENHART, Ella 19 James M 19 Veloy
Pearl 19
ELSEY, Charles Eugene 7 Samuel 7
EMMERLING, John C 40 Margaret 40
ENDLEY, Lavina 10 Lemuel 10 William
Pore 10
EPLEY, Adaline 14 Angeline 14 Charles
Newton 14 William A 14
ESWINE, Charels 51 Charles 51 Martha J
51
EUKE, Ada 33 Ferdinand 33 Nellie
Florence 33
EVANS, Armsford 47 Bessie V 8 C D 8
Charles E 10 Charles Harrison 47
Columbus D 8 Gertrude P 7 Grace 25
Harry Bradshaw 10 Isanthus L 25 James
B 10 John E 25 John G 7 Joseph D 25
Laura 47 Mary Rebecca 25 Minerva
Frances 8 Rachel B 7 Rosa B 25 Sarah D
10 Susanna 47 William E 47
EVERY, Anna Eliza 29 Edwin 29 Henry 29
EWING, Bishop 52 George 52 Margaret 52
FAGENBUSH, Estella G 7 Samuel K 7
FAHERTY, Agnes 29 Johanna 29 John 29
FARRELL, Lizzie O 32 Ruth 32
FARRINGTON, Ella 11 Mr 11 Mrs 11
Sadie 11
FAUCETT, Geneva 22 James L 22 Mattie
22
FAUCITT, James L 22 Mattie 22
FAUSITT, James L 22 Mattie 22
FELL, Almenia 17 John 17 William A 17
FENSTERMAKER, F M 27 Lulu 27
FERREL, Daisy Pickering 9 Jefferson 9
Laura J 9
FERRELL, Lizzie O 32 Ruth 32
FETTERS, Clyde 29 Mary A 29 Thomas J
29

FIDLER, George C 42 Irene 42 Nellie May
  Belle 42
FIELD, Lois 17
FIELDS, Blanche Fern 51 George W 47 51
  Ida 51 Ruth 47 Winifred Ruth 47
FILLER, Ada Ann 6 Eli 6
FINNEGAN, Bessie 47 Thomas 47
FITTRO, David 17 Emma 17 Mary 17
FITZPATRICK, William 4
FLAHERTY, Agnes 29 Johanna 29 John
  29
FLEMING, Alfretta M 52 Bell D 28
  Florence Catharine 33 Hugh B 28
  James 33 Kate 33 Katie 33 Nellie
  Marie 28
FORTNER, Myrtle 46
FOSTER, Elsie 25 Elsy 25 Etta 25 Lucy
  25 Wilson 25
FOURTH, May 42
FRISTOE, Mary E 2
FROHENBERG, Anna 34 Heinrich 34
  Henry 34 Katharina 34 Katharine 34
  Katie 34
FRY, Ida C 2 Margaretta C 2
GAINER, Mollie 14 Myrtle 14
GAINES, Mollie 14 Myrtle 14
GALVIN, Barbara 32 George 32 Grace A
  32
GANNAN, Dora 10 Henry F 10
GANNON, Dora 10 Henry F 10 Mary 10
GANON, Dora 10 Henry F 10 Mary 10
GARDNER, Myrtle 13
GARNER, Bell(e) 13 John S 1 2 Julia H 1
  2 Lenia Glendora 1 2 Lucille Gertrude
  45 Myrdia 13 Myrtle 13 Myrtle Belle 45
  William H 13
GASNELL, C F 51
GATTERDAM, Casper 19 Catharine 19
  Francisca 19
GAUER, Amelia Sophia 37 Mary K 37
  William J 37
GAUERE, Amelia Sophia 36
GEARY, Clara 25
GERMAIN, Sister Mary 22
GERMAINE, Sister Mary 22
GERRY, Clara 25
GERVAIS, Frank H 5 Mamie 5
GETREU, Alice 19 Edward 19 49 Frances
  49 Maud May 49 Thomas 19
GETRUE, Alice 19 Edward 19 Thomas 19
GIBBARD, Charles Allen 13 Joseph 13
  Laura A 13
GILBERT, Almira 12 Joseph Orlando 12
  Samuel B 12

GILL, Eleanor 3 George H 41 Hazel Mar-
  garet 41 Mamie M 41
GILLETT, Arthur 49 Mary 49 Ralph 49
GITHENS, Anna 46 Joseph 46 Mary 46
GOBLE, Chester William 35 Gardiner A
  35 Jennie A 35
GOODIN, Catharine 22 Fay Alice 22
  James 22
GORDON, Albert 2
GOSNELL, C F 51
GOULDNER, Frederick Lee 48 James
  Francis 48 Michael 48 Olive 48
GRAFF, Augustus B 10 Malissa 10 Wil-
  liam P 10
GRAHAM, Amos 15 Carla 38 Corda 38
  Floyd Lefler 38 Fred W 38 Orilla V 15
GRAY, Emma 28 Frances 3 Harriet 3
  Louisa 28 Samuel H 28
GREEN, Albert Orville 33 Alexander 22
  Maud(e) May 22 Ruth 22
GRIMES, Beatrice 18 Eliza 18 Jerry 18
GROOM, Emma Fern 37 Nettie 37 Sher-
  man 37
GROOMES, Edgar Palmer 37 Elijah H 37
  Mary 37
GROOMS, Edgar Palmer 37 Elijah H 37
  Mary 37
GROVES, Laura 34 Lura 34
GUERIN, Edward 31
GUNKLE, Bertha 28 Charley 28 Sophia 28
GURRIN, Edward 31
GURVIN, Edward 31
GUYER, Charles 35 Eleanor 35 Nora 35
HADDOCK, Clara 44 Roy 44
HAFER, Charles 15 Lucy Elizabeth 15
  Sarah 15
HAGART, Daniel 4 Daniel Thurman 4
HAINES, Jessie 35 John 35 Katie 35
HALL, Angie 12 Anna Mary 16 Charles 37
  Edna H 12 Henry M 3 Ida 3 John 12
  Judgie 19 Mary 3 Thomas 19 William W
  16
HANSBERY, Anna 50
HARDING, Kate B 47 Kate R 47 Violet
  Marie 47 William H 47
HARRIS, Emma Florence 28 Florence
  Louis 28 Joseph Edwin 28
HART, Raymond Bertrand 41 Sarah Jane
  41 Thomas 41
HARTEL, Mary 18
HAYES, Adeline 49 Camilla 5 Flora Elva
  5 John 5 Joseph 49
HAYS, Elizabeth 49 Thomas P 49
HEDRICK, Dennis E 43 Lorhetta May 43

HEDRICK (continued)
  Lulu May 43
HEINIG, Emma 7 Valentine 7
HENNEKE, Amelia 21 Amelia 22 Barbara
  21 22 Detrick 21 22 Henry 21 22 Kate
  21
HENNEKER, Amelia 21
HENNIS, Clara B 41 Edward L 41 Joseph
  Leo 41
HENRY, Georgiana 1 Mary 1 William S 1
  2
HERMAN, Bessie Maria Mc Mellen 17
  Charlotte A 17 John F 17
HERSHISER, Mattie 51
HESSE, Adolf John 27 Armie 27 Lester
  Adolf 27
HIGGINSON, Gertrude B 40 John 40 Mary
  A 40
HILDEBRAND, Isaac K 7 Mary J 7
HILL, Mary 46 Mr 46 Mrs 46
HILLS, Brainerd D 12 Clarence Clare 12
  Mary S 12
HILTEBRAND, Isaac K 7 Mary J 7 Polly
  7
HINDS, John 50 Ruby Rosella 50
HISCHKE, Anna Greta 29 Fred 29
  Frederick Herman 35 Johanna 29
  Johannah 35 Katie 36
HITE, Charles E 33 Eva Goldie 33 Luella
  33
HOEFER, Amelia Sophia 37 Carrie 37
  Henry 37
HOLLAND, Alta May 11 Jane A 11
HOMET, Edna 31
HOMMEDIAN, Wallace H L 15
HOMMEDIEN, Bell L 15 Ethel L 15 Fred
  L 15 Wallace H L 15
HOMMENDIEN, Wallace H L 15
HORCH, Ervin 17 Howel 17 Mary 17
HORNET, Edna 31
HOUSTON, Alexander 2 Elizabeth Dunn 2
  Fannie Brooks 2 Jane 2
HOWE, Ada 47 Ada Helen 47
HUBER, Charles 50 Mabel L 50 Minnie 50
  William H 27
HUGHES, Minnie 47
HULL, Anna Mary 16 William W 16
HUMMERICH, Catherine 1 Catherine
  Elizabeth 1 Jacob William 1
HUTCHINS, Annie 12
HYLE, George Jefferson 25 May 25 Phil-
  lipanna 25
HYNE, George D 26 Hattie L 26
INGAL, Francis 24

INGALLS, Francis 24 Mary 24
JACKSON, Anna R 6 Avis 20 Carrie 6 El-
  len 27 F M 43 F W 43 Frank D 43 Helen
  27 James Y 20 Jennie E 43 Joe 20 John
  W 27 Joseph 3 Peter 39 Sarah A 20
  Susan 3 Virginia Elizabeth 43 Zoe Airs
  20
JAMES, Eva Maud 6 John 6 Martha E 6
JOERDING, Anna Louisa 36 Anna Maria
  36 Charlotte 36 Frederick 36
JOERGER, Anthony 46 Chester A 46
  Emma 46
JOHNSON, Ada B 32 Frank 51 Harry Lynn
  52 John W 32 Katharine 52 Rosana E 3
  Ruth 32 William Lynn 52
JOHNSTON, Alexander 13 Dora 21 Emily
  13 Mabel Eliza 21 Minnie 13
JOINER, Irene 19 Robert 19 Robert Huston
  19
JONES, Cora 39 Frank 21 Harry 39 Hattie
  21 John M 5 Julia Ann 47 Mary 42 Mary
  L 5 Nellie Leota 5 Peter 21 Wilie Julia
  47 William C 47
JORDON, Jackson 5 Leota 5 Mary E 5
JOYCE, Charles M 26 Chester 26 Mary F
  26
JUDSON, Anna 29 Ora 29
KARNES, John 22 John F 22 Odelia 22
KECK, Christopher 30 Ollivia 30 Phyllis
  Cornelia 30
KEHM, Edith N 42 Francis William 42
  George Jr 42
KELLER, Ella 39 John Joseph 39 Joseph
  10 Joseph L 39 Mary 10
KELLEY, Charlotte 25 Mary 50 Mendes
  50 Reuben 50 Wendes 50
KELLY, Anna Bell 51 Carrie C 51 Char-
  lotte 25 Florence C 43 George B 51
  Lawrence 43 Susan A 43 William E 43
KENNA, Polly 7
KENNEDY, Helen 24 Mary 23
KENT, 28
KERN, Anna M 40 Joseph F 40 Margaret
  Elsie 40
KERWOOD, Grace Ethel 45 Mary 45
KIEL, Anna 18 Beatrice 18
KILE, Mary Rebecca 25 William 25
KING, Bessie 34 Clarence L V 6 Robert
  34 Sallie 34
KINGRY, Edward Elijah 9 Lavetie Edna
  13 Rosetta M 9 13 Thomas 13 Thomas
  M 9 13
KINSER, Anna 27 Mary J 27
KINSEY, Roy H 51

KIRSCHNER, Adam 16 Clara 16
KLEINLEIN, Carrie 43 Wilbur David 43
    William 43
KNIRG, Clarence L V 6
KNODERER, Claira Belle 23 Maribel 23
    William A 23
KNOWLTON, Frank 10
KOEHLER, Anna 11 Charles 11 Matilda
    11 William 11
KOENIG, Helen 49 Katie 49
KOHLER, Charles 11 Matilda 11
KRELL, Charles 3
KRIM, Earl 42 Earl Dean 42 Jennie 42
    William C 42 William E 42
KRING, Clarence L V 6
KROGER, Anna 6 Harry Albert Richard 6
    John 6
KRUG, Clarence L V 6
KUEBRICH, Anna 11 August 11 Matilda
    11 William 11
KUEBRICK, Anna 11 William 11
LACEY, Rachael G 38
LACY, Mr 37 Mrs 37 Rachel 37
LALLAWAY, Maud 6 William 6
LAMAN, Alice 39 Rachel 39
LAMB, Annie 52 Arthur 52 Arthur C 52
LANG, Annie 19 Francis Nicholas 18
    George 45 Julia 45 Martin 19
LANGLOTZ, Frederika 1 Huldreich 1
    Mary Louisa 1
LANNING, Chester 52 Lena 52
LASHER, George 34 Lillie Ethel 34
    Malinda 34
LEFFINGWELL, Oliver R 6
LEFLER, Floyd 38
LEGER, Effie 41 Helen E 41 Michael 41
LEONARD, Catharine 6 Earl 18
LEW, C F 50 Catharine E 50 Frances
    Elizabeth 50
LEWIS, Bessie 51 David 7 Jennie Adams
    7 Mary D 7
LITCHFORD, Helen 27 Stella A 27
LLOYD, Mary Ann 3
LOCKE, George Martin 42 Martin G 42
    Mary A 42
LOEWER, Elizabeth 20 Mabel Elizabeth
    20 Valentine 20
LOWENS, Alice 23 Allice 23
LOWERS, Alice 23 Allice 23
LUCAS, Darius L 34 Minnie E 34 Nyra 34
LUCKS, Charles 9 Christiana 9
LYNAS, Elizabeth 25 James 25 May Hyle
    25
LYNN, Charles N 49 Katie 49 Ralph 49

MADDEN, Jennie 28 John 28
MAHONEY, Margaret 21
MAINES, Nannie Rockey 4
MALHEIM, Gertrude M 23
MALLAY, Dorah 4
MALONEY, Anna 9 John 9
MARTIER, Francis 22
MARTIN, Anna 15 Edward Rodney 15
    James E 15 Jennie C 26 John L 26
    Nellie Hazel 26
MASON, Joshua 2 Mary E 2 Nancy 2
MATHER, Horatio 31 Lillie Marie 31
    Mary 31
MAY, Edith 47 Nellie 36
MC CORMICK, Clarence 40 Frank 40
    Mattie 40
MC DONALD, William Anderson 13
MC DONNEL, Cora 45 John 45 Minnie
    May 45
MC DOWELL, Alenson 39 Anna 39 Annie
    39 Ethel 39
MC EWEN, Anna Carlisle 12 Goldie 12
    William S 12
MC GUIRE, Patrick 6
MC KENNA, Alexander 47 Louisa 47 Os-
    car Earl 47
MC MELLEN, Bessie Maria 17
MC MILLEN, Bessie Maria 17 Eva 42
    Solomon H 17
MC NALLY, Alice 20
ME MILLEN, Charlotte A 17
MEACHAM, Edward Elijah 9 Elijah 9
    Mary E 9
MEALHEIM, Clara 23 Gertrude M 23
MEALHIEM, Clara 23 Gertrude M 23
MEALHIEN, Gertrude M 23
MEINSEN, Henry 15 Mary 15 William H
    15
MEINSON, Henry 15 Mary 15 William H
    15
MENELE, Adelia 9 Amelia 9
MENELEY, Adelia 9 Amelia 9
MENGER, Frances 37 Mary 37 Patrick 37
MEREDITH, Charles R 20 Mary A 20
    Saddie 20
MESSMER, James 20 Joseph 20 Mollie 20
MICKEL, Isabella 8 James 8 Minnie
    Frances 8
MILLAY, Dorah 4 Philip 4 William 4
MILLER, Charles Henry 30
MINER, Ann 13 Earl D 18 Eli D 18
    Lavestie Edna 13 Mary E 18 Samuel L
    13
MINNICK, Edna P 31 J Ed 31 Mary 31

MINOR, Earl D 18 Eli D 18 Mary E 18
MITCHELL, Jennie 28 Maud 28
MOEHL, Jennie E 30 John Henry 30 Sylvia Celia 30
MOEHM, Abraham 26 Emma 26
MOEHN, Abraham 26 Emma 26 Harrold 26
MOGAN, Emmit 31
MOITIER, Francis 22
MOORE, Eliza N 23 Harry 5 Helen 24 Margaret 5 Solomon S 24
MORAN, Alice Delaney 29 Mary 29 May 29 Michael 29
MOREHEAD, Eva May 10
MOREHEAN, Susan A 10
MORGAN, Emmil 31 Mary Jane 31
MORTNER, Francis 22
MOSS, Mary F 49 Maud May 49 Theodore T 49
MUELLER, Louise 15 William 15
MURPHY, 1
MUTISPAUGH, Charles 31 Mary 31
MYERS, Benjamin R 8 Ebenezer 8 George H 39 Ida D 39 Mary E 8 Otto 39
NAGEL, Pearl 30
NAGLE, George M 30 John H 30 Josephine 30 Pearl 30 Virginia 30
NASH, Estella 6
NEISWANDER, Ella 38
NEUNER, Carl Otto 36 Christopher 36 Marie L F 36
NEWTON, Denny H 42 Homer Ellsworth 42 Mary 42 Mary Elizabeth 42
NICKEL, Isabella C 8 James 8 Minnie Frances 8
NICKELSON, Angelina 4 Thurman 4
NIENKIRCHEN, Clarence Louis 28 Ellen 28 John L 28
NOBLE, Elmira 6
NORTON, Nellie May 36 Susanna 36 William 36
OARE, Malinda 46 47 Sanford Brownlee 46 William 46 47 Winnie Marie 47
OBR, Anna C 41
OGLE, Anna E 33 Wesley H 33
OKEY, Dorothy 29 Inez 29
ORB, John V 41 Mary A 41
ORMES, Ada Belle 43 Virgie 43
OVERBECK, Almeda C 51 Doris Lydia Elizabeth 51 Joseph G 51
PAGE, Leonard S 34 Mabel Beatrice 34 Mary C 34
PAINE, Odra May 45 Olive 45 William M 45

PALMER, Eliza Ruth 14 Homer 37 Lucy Elizabeth 14 Mary 14 William Francis 14
PARISH, Emeroy 42 Ethel 42 Torrence J 42
PARKER, Mary 17
PARSONS, Marie Alice 23 Maude 23 Nanie 23
PATNO, Frank 38 William 38 Willie 38
PATTERSON, Angeline 14 Charles Epley 14 Effie Levisa 10 Effie Levitha 10 Mary V 10 Philip D 10 Robert 14
PAYNTER, Florence Ruth 48 John F 48 Mary 48
PECKHAM, Katharine Agnes Clark 45 Mary A 45 Richard M 45
PERDUE, Blanche 20 Catharine 20 Cornelius 20
PETERMAN, Kate 21 Mabel Eliza 21 Samuel 21
PETTICORD, Amos W 18 Dora Mabel 18 Samantha C 18
PHILLIPS, Anna 25 Jesse 25 Maria 25 Olive 25 Oliver 25
PHIPPS, Ella 48 Lulu May Jefferson 48
PICKERING, Daisy May 9 Jennie 9 Sylvanus Wood 9
PINNEY, Henrietta 41 Ida J 30 Ida M 41 Ida T 30 Justin 30 41 Maud 10 Nathan 41 Pheny Gorden 30 William 10
PITTELKOW, Benjamin R 8 Herman C 8 Valetta 8 Vialitta 8
PITTON, Bertha 8 Mary 8 Philipp 8
PLATT, Augustus 7 Charles E 7 Ruth S 7
POLLEY, Emma 44 Roy 44 Seymore 44
PORTER, Doris 37 Elaine M 37
POTTER, Alfred 40 Clara Esther 40 Delia M 40 Della M 40 Janetta 14 Peter 14 Sarah 14
PRETTYMAN, Charles 38 Dora 38 Harry 38
PRICE, Clara Belle 19 Ella 22 Eugene 40 John C 19 John E 22 John Karnes 22 Lillian 40 May 19
QUIMBY, Adaline H 7 George A 7 Jennie 7
RADLEY, Joseph 12
RAFFERTY, Marie Stanslus 44 Mary A 44 Michael J 44
RANDALL, Annie E 12 Florence Mabel 12 John W 12
RANEY, Oliver 23
RANGER, Mary E 32 Nathen 50 Walter 32 William H 32

RANNEY, John Frank 23 Louisa 23 Oliver 23

READ, Drusius B 21 Mena L 21 Nellie A 21

REASONER, Elmer 38 John 38 Mary 38

REDMAN, Anna 10 Belle 20 Bessie Adelline 24 Eva May 10 Henrietta 20 John T 20 Julia 20 Mary E 20 Samuel 24 Sandusky 24

REENS, Bertha 49 Jasper 49 John 49

REITER, Anna 51 Frank 51 Henry 51

REMINGTON, Almira 12 Joseph Orlando 11 Oscar 12

RICE, James 1 Jeremiah 1 Mary Ann 1

RICHARDSON, Aaron P 7 Adaline 7 Sarah J 7

RICKENBACHER, Frederick 17 John 17

RINEHART, Ada Ann 6 Emma A 6 John 6

RITTER, Lula 51 Lulu 51 Ruth 51

ROBINSON, Mabel 8 Mable 8

ROBY, Minnie May 45

ROCHE, Francis Nicholas 19 Margaret 19 Nicholas 19

ROCKWELL, DeWitt 16 28 Fannie Mary 28 Isabel 16 Jennie Bell 16 Mary 28

RODERICK, Charles 37 Dora Adella 37 Nanna 37

RODGERS, Julia 5 Mary 5

ROEDELSBERGER, Frank 26 Lizzie 26 Peter 26

ROVER, Jacob K 5

ROYCE, D H 1 2 Lenia Glendora 1 2 Sallie A 1 2

RUBY, Cora 35 45 John 35

RUCKMAN, James 19

RUSH, Anna C 41 John L 41 Mary C 41

RUSK, Eliza Jane 3 James B 3 William 3

RYAN, Agness 29 Bessie Adeline 24 Ellen 2 Ida Elizabeth 2 Jane 24 John 29 Sarah 29

SAGER, Charlie W 12 John T 12 Mary 12

SAGSETTER, John T 41

SAGSTETTER, John T 41 Joseph Leo 41 Magdalena 41

SANDS, Dolly 16 Harriet 16 Joseph 16

SAVIERS, Clara Belle 23 Columbus D 23 Maribel Phyllis 23

SCANLAN, Bartholomew 3 Margaret 3

SCHENCK, Anna 34 John 34 Katharina 34 Katie 34

SCHMELTZ, Fred 18 Jerome 18 Laura 18 Louisa 18

SCHMIDT, Carl 10 Charles 10 Emilie 10 Joseph 10

SCHNEIDER, Charles L 30 Eda Elizabeth 2 Elizabeth M 2 Flora A 30 Florence 32 Grace 32 Jacob 32 John William 2 Pauline Adele 30

SCHREINER, Gertrude B 40 Jacob A 40 Mary A 40

SCOTT, Bertha 24 Harry 27 John Wallace 27 Percy 24 Rosey Fender 27 Rosey Leander 27 William 24

SELBY, Edward 33 Helena Lucile 33 Lillian M 33

SELLEY, Edith May 47

SELLY, Florence 47

SENDELBACH, Andrew 23 Mary Josephine 23 Minnie J 23

SHARP, Julia Elizabeth 19

SHAW, Graham 49 John H 49 Lottie 49

SHEAF, Emma E 26 Hellie 26

SHEEHAN, Silvia Celia 30 Sylvia Celia 30

SHERA, Dora A 39 Elizabeth C 39 Frank D 39 lillian 39

SHIPE, Ida 15 Lydia 15

SHOTTS, Effie 4 Jennie 4 William J 4

SHREEVES, James H 20 Joe Avis 20 Sarah A 20

SHRIEVES, Lee Fay 32 Martha 31 Thomas E 31

SHRIVES, Lee Fay 32 Martha 31 Thomas E 31

SHROCK, Dela 26 George Harrold 26 John 26

SIBLEY, Amanda M 26 Chester 26 Henry H 26

SIMMS, May 21

SIMPKINS, Florence Anna 36 Georgiana 36 W S 36

SIMPSON, Charles E 16 Edmund 16 Emma F 16 Harriet 16 Harriet S 16

SINES, Daisy E 50 Maggie 50

SINNS, May 21

SKELTON, John B 5 Julia 5 Mary A 5

SMELTZER, Albert John 9 Charles 9 Minnie 9

SMITH, 31 Adelia A 9 Amanda 9 Clarence 40 Edmund 16 George B 23 Herny 9 Jennie V 16 Katie 30 Lucy M 23 Mary 40 Mary Ethel 23 Rush 16

SMULLEM, F M 34 Mabel Beatrice 34 Mabele Beatrice 34 Mable Beatrice 34 Mary C 34

SNYDER, Charles H 38 Mildred 38 Roby Dell 38

SOKOFF, Ida 46 John 46 Sanford Brownlee 46

SOPHAR, Amanda 10 William 10
SOPHER, Amanda 10 Maud 10 William 10
SPADE, Bessie Edith 8 Daisie 8 Henry W
   8 Lucy A 8
SPAFFORD, Alice 10
SPANGLER, Amanda 23 Fillmore 23
   George D 23 Mary Ethel 23 William 23
SPENCER, Fredie 15
SPINDLER, Catharine 50 J A 50 John Al-
   bert 50
SPITLER, Florence C 43 Ida V 43 W G 43
   William E 43
SPRAGUE, Blanche 20 Ella F 20 Oscar 20
STAFFORD, Louisa 24 Percy Scott 24
STAGER, Caroline 21 Frank 21
STAGG, Amanda 43 John 43
STAGGS, Ada Belle 43 Amanda 43 John
   43
STEFFENS, Edward 15 Fredie 15 Rosetta
   15
STEFFIN, Edward 15 Fredie 15 Rosetta
   15
STEWART, Annabel G 40 Giles 40 Helen
   40
STILTZ, Frances Elizabeth 49 Oleveya 50
STINE, Cora Margaretta 23 George W 23
   Jennie M 23
STINSON, James 20 James Jr 20 Kate 20
STOCKDALE, Grace 32 Nancy L 32
   Richard D 32
STRIMPLE, Ada R 46 John W 46 Thelma
   Ellis 46
STUMP, Blanch Edna 37 Blanche Edna 37
   Emmet N 37 Eva May 37
SURELL, Joseph 52 Martha 52
SURRELL, Bishop Ellsworth 52 Joseph 52
   Martha 52
SUYDAM, Helen 40 Myra A 40
SWALLEY, Florence 46
SWANK, James 48 Sarah L 48
SWARBRICK, Alice Jane 22 John Thos 22
   Richard 22 William 22
SWEENEY, Mary 18 S D 18
SWELLY, Edith May 47 Florence 47
SWENY, MARY 15 S D 15
SWICKARD, Doris 43 Joshua 43 Russell
   43 Sarah 43
SWITZER, Charles Harrison 47 Frank 47
   Minnie Hughes 47
TAYLOR, Charles 3 Electa 3 Ella 41
   Helen 41 Nellie 32 Nelly 32 William 3
TEVLIN, Lottie 47 Oscar Earl 47 Patrick
   47
THALER, Margaretha 26 Paulus 26

THOMAS, Harry 44 Maud 44 William 44
THOMPSON, David J 15 Jennette S 15
   Nellie 41 Olive Gertrude 15 William 41
THROCKMORTON, Maggie 17 Mary 17
TIPTON, Alice Marie 39 Mary C 39 O D
   39
TRACEY, Carrie 19 Robert 19
TROTT, Caroline 31 Peter 31
UHRICH, Fredericka 13 Minnie 13 Philip
   13
ULLRICH, Minnie 13
ULRICH, Fredericka 13 Philip 13
URY, Edward J 38 Elmer 38 Florence 38
VATH, John Anton 21 Josette 21
VINCANT, Lillie Marie 31 Margaret 31
VINT, Lila Bessie 34 Lydia A 34 Richard
   H 34
VOGT, Charles 5 Helena 5 Peter 5
VOLK, Lucille Gertrude 45 Nellie 45 Wil-
   liam F 45
WADKINS, Angie 50
WAGNER, Franklin H 46 Mary N 46
   Nancy J 46
WALCUTT, Jennie Bell 16
WALLEY, Jane 18 John 18 John H 18
WALSH, Frances Bell 6 John 6 Josephine
   6
WALTON, Addie 12 Edna H 12 Lucius 12
WARD, Ella 50 Harry 50 Lillian 50
WARE, Doris Nevada 37 Mrs H F 37
WATSON, Francis J 18 Minnie F 18
   Samuel W 18
WEIDEL, N W 48
WEIDENKOPF, Andrew 1 Elizabeth 1
   Gertrude 1 Margaret/Margaretha 1
WEIDLE, Frederick Virgil 48 Nicholas 48
WEINLAND, Ellen 46 J A 46 Mary 46
WHARTON, Elizabeth 2 Fannie B 2 Jane
   2 Robert J 2
WHITE, Mabel 27
WIGGINS, Amelia 21 Mary Leila 21 Wil-
   liam 21
WILL, John Joseph 39 Mary E 39 Wil-
   liam A 39
WILLEKE, Barbara 38 Charles E 38
   Frederick C 38 John Frederick 38 Mary
   Elizabeth 38 William Joseph 38
WILLIAMS, Frank 25 George C 31 George
   Clyde 31 Hattie 36 Jennie 25 Lemuel E
   36 Lillie 25 Lizzie Dell 31 Lizzie Dill
   31 Martha Fay 36 Oliver P 36
WILSON, Frank 51 George W 33 Harley J
   33 J 1 James 1 Lydia 1 May 33 Rhoda
   51

WING, Howard Everett 4 Mary M 4 William H 4
WINNING, Annie 12 James 12 Pearl Anderson 12
WINSTAFFER, Lawrence 14 Loren 14 Sarah E 14 Thomas Williard 14
WINWARD, Alexander 22 William Swarbrick 22
WOLCOTT, Jennie Bell 16 Kate 16 Rheal 16
WOLCUTT, Jennie Bell 16 Kate 16 Rheal 16
WOLF, Anna E 38 Margaret A 38 Peter H 38 Willie 38
WOLFEL, Ethel Lina 44 Julia 44 William H 44
WOLFREY, Arthur W 36 Dewitt Tallmadge 36 Margaret F 36
WOOD, Bertie Leota 51 C R 53 Clyde R 53 Cullen 51 Sarah 51

WOODSIDE, Mary Leila 21 Stella 21
WOOLLEY, Fannie 34 Harold Dean 34 Solomon J 34
WORCESTER, James F 35 Jane 35
WRIGHT, C J 48 Emma 28 Henry 28 Lulu Phipps 48 Lydia 28 Martha 48
WUEST, John 5
WYLIE, Frank E 27 Frank M 27 Ida J 27
YEMMANS, Chas 51
YENMANS, Chas 51
YOCUM, George 47
YOUNG, Albert C 30 Anna 46 Clarence Adel 30 Georgiana 1 2 Hannah Charlotte 1 Leona May 46 William H 46 Zina M 30
ZETTLER, Elizabeth 17 Joseph Bernard 17 Paul Bethge 17